Contents

Introduction

The Cleverness of Boys was first conceived some time after the publication of our book *Boys and Girls Come out to Play* (Featherstone), and was inspired by the discussions we had with the many parents, practitioners and teachers who attended conferences on the issues of gender in the early years. It soon became evident that in order to inform the debate about young boys, we needed to write a book that just focused on boys.

Many boys, particularly those from age three to seven who are attending full-time out-of-home care in the UK, are seen to be failing to thrive. They are sometimes falling into the spiral of low self-esteem, low levels of achievement and unacceptable behaviour that blights their time in school and can affect their whole lives. Boys feel frustrated, angry and unappreciated. Adults swing between feelings of irritation, fury and pity, as they try to understand the minds and behaviours of the boys in their care. We felt that there was a need to draw together the latest information about brain development and behaviour, and to suggest ways in which we might all begin to understand the issues faced by boys in our twenty-first century homes, settings and schools.

This book is unashamedly about boys. It encourages the reader to recognise how talented and capable boys really are, and attempts to show a way forward for us all in recognising their cleverness and talents.

In discussing with colleagues the content of this book, we realised that there are many different views on the difference between boys and girls and how we, as adults, can help boys in particular to succeed when their early years in education are dominated by women. Of these many views, three seem to predominate.

Are boys and girls the same?

One view says, 'There is no difference between boys and girls, so we should treat them exactly the same and have the same expectations of everyone'. This view supports the position of equality, of treating everyone the same (which of course we would all support), where both girls and boys are encouraged to play with dolls, build with construction kits, play football, dress up, climb trees and so on. If we do this, the theory is that children will grow up with the same characteristics and behaviour, emerging as strong, caring, energetic, talkative people. Our opinion is that the 'equality at all costs' view, while a

The
CLEVERNESS
of Boys

Sally Featherstone and Ros Bayley

'Peter, boylike, was indifferent to appeara es, and about in the wildest glee. Alas, he had ady forgotten that he owe to Wendy. He thought he had attached the shadow (to his foot) himself. "How clever I am," he crowed rapturously. "Oh, the cleverness of me!" It is humiliating to have to confess that this conceit of Peter was one of his most fascinating qualities.'

Peter Pan by J M Barrie

Reprinted 2010
Published 2010 by A&C Black Publishers Limited
36 Soho Square, London W1D 3QY
www.acblack.com

ISBN 978-1-4081-1468-1

Text © Ros Bayley and Sally Featherstone 2010
Design © Bob Vickers 2010

A CIP record for this publication is available from the British Library.

The authors and publishers are grateful for permission to reproduce the following:
p.15: From The Blank Slate by Steven Pinker. Reproduced by permission of Steven Pinker;
p.64: From The Growth of Independence in the Young Child by J Bowlby. Reproduced by
permission of the Royal Society of Health Journal; p 79: From Growing Great Boys by Ian
Grant. Reproduced by permission of Random House Vermillion; p 90 From Environments for
Play by Theresa Casey. Reproduced by permission of Play Scotland; pp 93: From Preschool-
Aged Children's Television Viewing in Child Care Settings by Dimitri A Christakis and
Michelle M. Garrison. Reproduced by permission of Pediatrics. p 103: From Determinants of
Aspirations by Leslie Morrison and Rodie Akerman. Reproduced by permission of the
Institute of Education.

Every effort has been made to trace copyright holders and to obtain their permission for use of
copyright material. The authors and publishers would be pleased to rectify any error or
omisson in future editions.

Printed in Great Britain by Latimer Trend & Company Limited

This book is produced using paper that is made from wood grown in
managed, sustainable forests. It is natural, renewable and recyclable.
The logging and manufacturing processes conform to the environmental
regulations of the country of origin.

To see our full range of titles
visit www.acblack.com

worthy aim, has not worked. Being politically correct has disadvantaged everyone because equal does not mean that everyone is the same. The principle which replaced 'to each according to their need' with 'everyone should have the same', has let everyone down.

The vast majority of parents and education professionals will say this view can no longer be supported. They spend their days working and playing with both boys and girls, and they know that boys and girls are different; that even when you take away race, colour and religion, boys and girls behave differently, are interested in different things and are switched on to learning in different ways. Watch children in a park, garden, classroom or nursery and the differences are apparent. Early years practitioners asked if there is any difference will say *yes* and so will parents who particularly comment on the differences between siblings when the first and subsequent children are of different sexes.

So we think it is time to recognise that each individual boy and girl has different needs, behaviours and strengths. Recognising these and working to meet them will help us to ensure that every child is treated as the unique being they are, and that with real equality of *opportunity* to access individualised support, they can achieve their potential.

Are sex and gender the same thing?

A second view is that *sex* and *gender* are the same thing, making all boys the same and all girls the same. This view says that boys are masculine, girls are feminine and we should keep it that way by having specific and different expectations of boys and girls. They may say, 'Boys will be boys, all action, violence and fidget. All girls are quiet, sensitive and willing to sit still'. In this camp may sit the people who talk about 'man flu' and 'multitasking'. They may have read the book *Men are from Mars Women are from Venus* (Thorsons), and spend their personal and professional lives making simplistic judgements, justified by their extreme point of view, even if this may not fit the individual they are looking at.

But what about the boy who is caring and sensitive, the girl who loves football, the boy who learns to talk and read at an early age, or the girl who has difficulty sitting still? How can we explain this if we think that sex and gender are the same thing? There are feminine boys and masculine girls, as demonstrated by artistic and creative TV presenters such as Lawrence Llewellyn Bowen and extreme risk takers like Ellen MacArthur who has twice sailed around the world alone.

One could describe the difference by saying: 'Sex is in your underwear and gender's in your brain', clearly differentiating between the physical differences connected with our sexuality and the behavioural ones which are located in our brains.

There is now certainly enough evidence from brain research to convince us as writers that there really are differences between male and female brains, and that the differences are even greater than the differences between the sexes. Of course, the gender spectrum combined with the range within each of the sexes means that there are probably more differences *across* the feminine spectrum and the masculine spectrum than there are between males and females.

The influence of nature, nurture and culture

And then there's the third debate, which is the ongoing discussion about the influence of 'nature', 'nurture' and 'culture' on human behaviour and development. Opinion has swung between such extremes as, 'It's all in the genes' (the nature view) or 'It's all in the parenting' (the nurture view) or 'It's society's fault' (the culture view).

Over recent decades people have developed theories where nature, nurture or culture were considered to have the greatest influence on what children are and become. These theories include: boys are late readers solely because their fathers were late readers, girls are caring because they have watched their mothers with their younger siblings, aggression in young boys is something we can put down to a violent culture or too much TV.

Such theories, backed up by the knowledge and opinion of the age have left a trail across the centuries of competing views of the proportional influence of nature, nurture and culture. These range from the concept that babies are 'blank slates for us to write on' to the idea that we are entirely influenced by the family or society we happen to experience.

How can a single influence produce such different results? If it is all in the nurture, how can identical twins, reared in different families far apart from each other, and not even aware of their twin's existence, grow up to like the same food, have the same mannerisms and even choose the same clothes? If it is all in the nature, how can two brothers be so different when they have the same parents and genetic code, live in the same house and go to the same school? If it is all due to culture, why is it that most boys, regardless of the culture of their youth, grow up to be reasonable members of society?

New evidence

New evidence continues to shape our views, influenced by science, anthropology and psychological studies. Steven Pinker now proposes the following balance in humans of:

- nature (around 50%)
- nurture (not more than 10%)
- chance, including culture (around 50%).

This extreme and unusual view of the nature/nurture/culture balance (which also adds up to more than 100%!) confounds all previous views. It gives massive weight to genetic make-up, which is constantly shaped and reformed by the chances of individual lives, such as health, pre-natal influences, exposure to hormones, viruses, accidents and events over which we have little or no control. The reduction in the influence of family and nurture comes as a bit of a shock, particularly to those of us who spend our lives working to support parents in the upbringing of their children. However, when given thoughtful consideration, it begins to help us understand why we end up like we do – creatures of chance, each fashioned on a genetic framework, but constantly buffeted by events that change the direction of our development.

What we, as authors and lifetime 'boy watchers' believe, is that the *third way*, a way that recognises every boy (and every girl) as a unique mixture of nature, nurture and chance is the nearest we have found to what we see and what parents, practitioners and children themselves tell us. Boys are creatures of nature, nurture and chance, with different strengths and needs, influenced in different ways, their personalities shaped by chance, so they are different, not just from girls, but even from brothers in the same family, born of the same parents.

The purpose of this book

We also know, as parents, practitioners and teachers tell us time and time again about these differences, that boys *do* have different needs, and that mothers and female practitioners often find boys a mixture of mystery, puzzle, frustration and wonder. These people ask us for help, guidance, and particularly for information about the unique differences of boys, and that is the purpose of this book. We have tried to find out all we can about the intrinsic nature of boys, and we present this for your consideration.

We have constructed chapters about the current culture and why children, and boys in particular, are under pressure. We have attempted to unscramble the latest research on male and female brains, how they are similar and how they seem to be different, and how gender balance can complicate boys' lives and their life chances. And finally, we look at stories of individual boys, each one unique, each of them clever in different ways.

We have chosen to call the unique abilities, skills, interests and behaviours of boys 'clevernesses', a reference to a very clever and self-assured boy – Peter Pan. We explore the clevernesses through the stories of eight boys, each one giving us a unique challenge, both professionally and personally. The stories have been collected over time, and describe real boys in real schools and settings, with real adults and real families.

At the end of each story we have tried to describe the characteristics of each boy, why they behave as they do, think as they do and relate to others as they do. We show how their parents, practitioners and friends supported them to become the best boys they could be, not by pressing them into some pre-ordained mould, but by responding to their uniqueness in ways that suit their complex personalities. Each chapter has some guidance on ways to support boys who are like them, ways that suit boys' brains and bodies, that take into account their gender, genes and their specialisms, not just their sex.

We have spent much time on reading and research, observation and discussion of the needs and natures of boys. We have tried to read both wisely and widely, in books, research reports, magazines and learned articles. We have been influenced by:

- findings from the Human Genome Project (the latest on the nature of our genetic make-up);
- findings and reports of brain scientists and researchers (to understand the latest information about the structure of the brain);
- the work of developmental and behavioural psychologists from a range of viewpoints (to explore behaviour and child development);
- books on the development of children's bodies and brains (to be sure that we balance the work of great thinkers of the past with current literature on learning, thinking and growing).

We have also read and re-read the extensive writings of those who have studied boys and their needs over many years, adapting their guidance and views in the light of the latest research.

We hope that what we have produced is thoughtfully presented and thought-provoking for the reader. We have decided not to complicate the text with footnotes and reference numbers. Instead, we have given readers an extensive book and resources list at the end of the book, leaving the boys and their stories to stand for themselves.

Sally Featherstone and Ros Bayley

Nature, nurture, culture and chance

The nature/nurture debate has been with us for several centuries and opinion has swung wildly during this time, influenced by world events, philosophy and, more recently, by research on the growth of the human brain.

This is a short review of the progress of the discussion and we leave you to decide where you stand as we all move into the first half of the 21st century. Whatever you think about the debate, and this may be influenced by religion, philosophy, politics or your own circumstances, we can no longer look at the boys in this book, or the boys in our lives, without giving some thought to the issues covered in this chapter.

The nature/nurture debate

Thomas Hobbes in the early 17th century promoted the view in *Leviathan*, that humans are all savage by nature, that '...the life of man is solitary, poor, nasty, brutish and short', implying that the only way to manage society was through policing and constant discipline. Of course, this view affected child-rearing practice and parenting, which was also heavy on discipline, and has stayed so until relatively recent times.

John Locke in the 17th century introduced the idea of the 'blank slate' or 'empty vessel', describing the brain at birth as a 'tabula rasa', ready to be filled with knowledge. This viewpoint still has its supporters – it is the job of parents and society to fill the slate with behaviours, morals and intelligence. The nurture philosophy was born here, and has seen some extremes where dictatorship has used the blank slate theory as an excuse for indoctrination.

Both the 'savage' and the 'blank slate' still have their followers, and the debate between nature and nurture has raged ever since.

In the 18th century Jean-Jaques Rousseau set out his philosophy of education in *Emile*, a work which challenged both Hobbes and Locke, and proffered the view of a different sort of savage, the 'noble savage'. This was a child who needed nature, simplicity and gentle support to enable him to fulfill his potential; not discipline, but freedom. Rousseau added to the debate by declaring that there is a natural goodness in children, which could be nurtured to achieve a different adulthood where aggression and 'nastiness' could be tempered by gentleness and 'nobility'.

This point of view still influences modern culture where 'natural is best', where we are bombarded by messages promoting organic food, natural childbirth, natural light, green living, and the notion of 'biophilia' where a love of nature, plants and the natural environment is paramount.

Even in the 20th century the influences of the nature/nurture debate have affected parenting styles, education policy and the culture in which we live. Some criminals blame their parents for their subsequent crimes, espousing the principle that parents and society are to blame for all the ills of their behaviour. The worst excesses of Equal Opportunities legislation in practice has implied that all children are equal (the same), not that all children have equal rights. Even the Geneva Convention on Human Rights, agreed in 1948 has not succeeded in removing the idea that equal treatment and opportunity is the same as *identical* treatment and opportunity. Just treating people as clones does not ensure fairness.

But does that mean that we have no control over the development of our children, that we have to adhere to either no influence or total influence, with parents, teachers and society as a whole swinging wildly between the nature and nurture views as we try to get it right?

Recent brain research

Brain research seems to have come to our rescue, and the current explosion of information from brain scans, from projects in tracking brain development, in looking at similarities and differences across and between brains, in worldwide research projects, and of course in the Human Genome Project is giving us some different possibilities to consider. They have been distilled for the lay reader here, and this will lead us into some generalisations. If you want to know more, use the wonders of the Internet and the Further Reading section (see page 126) to get started on your journey to forming *your* opinion.

There now appear to be more influences on children than we ever thought. Of course, there are the genes inherited from parents, and they will define certain characteristics. However, the Human Genome Project is exposing the detail of genetic structures and how they shape our lives. It now appears that genes are not fixed features of our inheritance. They can be switched on by life experiences and even by pure chance. The genetic features which 'switch on' autism, auto-immune conditions, allergies and many other illnesses and syndromes may be part of every one of us. The influences of life chances such as chemicals in our brains, accidents and illnesses may be capable of switching these genes on at any time.

Don Brown, Professor Emeritus of Anthropology at the University of California, has compiled a list of 300 Human Universals, '...those features of culture, society, language, behaviour and mind that, so far as the record has been examined, are found among all peoples known to ethnography and history'. Published in Steven Pinker, *The Blank Slate* (Viking Press 2002) The list includes attachment; the notion of baby talk; childhood fear of loud noises; critical learning periods; family (including women's major responsibility for childcare); male and female and adult and child seen as having different natures; jokes and insults; play and even toilet training and tickling. Of course in different cultures these features will look, sound and feel different, but what this work has done is to underline the fact that there is a complex patterning of the brain which is universal, and, certainly in research into animals, is present at birth.

The influence of upbringing and parenting has also been undermined when we look at the research on fraternal and identical twins, which indicates that even when twins are brought up by different parents, in different countries and following different religions, there is an amazing correlation between the patterns and functions of their brains. This can be seen in their behaviours, choice of clothes, and ways of talking. How can this happen if we subscribe to the nurture side of the debate, and not the nature side?

The place of chance

But nature is not all. One thing the Human Genome project must surely make us consider is the place of chance in influencing the culture of our upbringing, not only as individuals, but as societies. What influence can be attributed to a tsunami, exposure to drugs during pregnancy, a chance meeting with a superb teacher, or the everyday events that dog our lives and the lives of our children?

Steven Pinker in a lecture at the Massachusetts Institute of Technology (MIT) entitled 'The Blank Slate' argued that the balance between nature and nurture must now be adjusted to allow for culture (the culture of our families, friends and peer group), and the vast array of chances that may affect our growth and development.

His feeling, and it is one that is persuasive, is that **nature** (our genetic make-up) may have a huge effect on us, and as the Human Genome Project unfolds, this effect may prove to be even more significant. 'What these studies don't take into account is that parents provide their children with genes as well as an environment. The studies may be saying nothing more than that talkative people have talkative kids, violent people have violent kids, and sensible people have sensible kids.

When you redo the studies with the proper genetic controls, by studying twins or adoptees, the results are rather bracing.' 'The Blank Slate' by Steven Pinker in *The General Psychologist* (Spring 2006)

He goes on to explore the research on twins in some detail, uncovering the fascinating evidence that the brain structures and predispositions that we are born with are permanent patterns in our individual brains, even in twins separated at birth. In the video version of the MIT lecture, in answer to a question from the audience, Pinker proposes that parenting, or **nurture** may be almost insignificant when compared with **nature** and particularly with a third and previously unacknowledged factor – **chance**.

As parents, early years practitioners and teachers, we now need to triangulate our thoughts by taking this third factor into the debate, and recognising that this new element may well prove to be of an equal or even more important influence in children's lives. Of course, there will be differences in your view of the importance of chance in the lives of the boys and girls you work with, but you will know it is there for sure, whether you live and work in Wandsworth, Warrington or Windermere! The boys in this book are subject to these normal chances of birth, of parental relationships, of health and illness, of sibling position, of race and colour, but some have greater weight of chance in their lives – of family breakdown, of city living, of foster care, of parenting style.

Of course it might now be easy to say, 'If there's nothing I can do, and everything is now up to a combination of nature and chance, does it matter what I do to, for or with these children? I could love them, abuse them, or ignore them, and it wouldn't make any difference'. Well, the answer is that we do have a responsibility, and that is to ensure that of the 300 Human Universals, we should **nurture** the ones that will support the child, recognise and understand the unique **nature** of each one, and do what we can to mitigate against the **chances** that undermine their development while recognising and building on those which could help them.

This book is about just that!

The growth of the brain in boys and girls

The chance of life

At the moment of conception some very significant and permanent things are decided. Among these must surely be the genetic influence of both parents, and how dominant and recessive genes make certainties of such characteristics as eye colour. The first random chance event for each of us is the decision our parents made to mate and take the chance of a child as a result. For all sorts of reasons, that chance may have been carefully considered or not considered at all, and for each of us the first random event of a randomised life was where and into which family we would be born.

The next chance could be described as the throwing of a thousand dice, the dice of our genes, which, as soon as we were conceived began to react to the environment in which it found itself. This involved processing chemicals in our mother's body, marshalling cells to grow into the constituent parts of a human body and switching on programmes for developing bone, muscle, eyes and fingers. These dice fall into the pattern of our magical DNA, spiralling through our chromosomes, each of which is replicated in every cell in our body. One of these dice determines our sex – it has an F on three sides and an M on the other three. If your dice fell with the M upwards, you will have an X and a Y chromosome in each cell; if your dice fell with an F upwards, you will have two X chromosomes. The Y chromosome has been called the 'genetic master switch' for converting embryos into males.

The effect of foetal testosterone

Another of the thousand dice has 'testosterone' stamped on it. This dice determines your sensitivity to testosterone throughout your body, including within your brain. A strong reaction to testosterone will make you more restless, aggressive and focused on action. As testosterone affects the brain and triggers the production of cortisol, this may make you less able to control your actions, words, or feelings. A weaker reaction to testosterone will make you more likely to respond to oestrogen, this may make you calmer, more likely to be interested in people and more able to control your impulses. This factor in your life is another chance, and boys will usually have a higher sensitivity to testosterone than girls.

When you combine the testosterone dice with your 'sex' dice, the one that destines you for life as a male or a female, then you have a primed trigger, which will place you on a gender spectrum containing typically 'masculine' behaviours and typically 'feminine' behaviours. A high sensitivity to testosterone and a male sexuality will place you at the extreme masculine end of the spectrum; a low sensitivity to testosterone and a female sexuality will place you on the feminine end of the spectrum.

Of course, most of us are a mixture of these types, and are scattered along the gender spectrum in wide variety, with some girls nearer to the masculine end and some boys nearer to the feminine end. These girls are not destined to be lesbians (although some may be), any more than the boys are destined for homosexuality. The girls may become scientists, sportswomen, business executives or explorers. The boys may become poets, social workers, painters or psychologists. One thing we do know is that there is more overlap between femininity and masculinity than there is difference:

'The topic of gender differences has been hotly debated in professional circles. First of all there are many more differences among children of the same sex than between the sexes. If we lined up all the boys and all the girls on the basis of almost any characteristic, there would be lots more overlap than difference attributable only to gender. Nevertheless, two important strands of research are confirming what parents have known all along: Overall, boys and girls prefer different activities and excel at different skills. They may even think differently. Much of this variation is clearly due to environmental factors, but some of it reflects biological variation in brain organisation.' Jane M Healy, *Your Child's Growing Mind* (Broadway Books 1987)

However, as Jane Healy says, there are differences too, and recent research indicates that '...as of 2005, scientists have identified more than one hundred structural differences between the brains of girls and boys'. Michael Gurian, *Nurture the Nature* (Jossey Bass 2009)

We now know that every foetus starts life as a 'default' female, that is, unless something happens to change it, every baby will become a girl. However, between weeks 14 and 16, bursts of testosterone begin to flood the foetus. Some of the testosterone is produced by the foetus, some by the mother. Foetuses destined to be boys (those with the Y chromosome) produce up to two and a half times as much as girls, and as far as we now know, the loaded trigger of sensitivity to this foetal testosterone results in both sex and gender differences. Sex is certainly determined at this stage, and probably the position on the gender spectrum is too.

The Cleverness of Boys

Work following the Human Genome Project now indicates that this period is also critical in triggering other tendencies, particularly characteristics described as 'masculine' such as an interest in organising and categorising things. There also seem to be newly discovered possibilities that the testosterone burst can trigger genetic problems such as autism, stuttering and dyslexia, and that all these problems are more common in boys and men.

One thing that is known is that foetal testosterone does encourage the growth of the right hemisphere of the brain, and depress the growth of the left side. Add this to the fact that simultaneously, boy babies are changing their bodies from 'default' female to male, moving their sexual organs from the insides of their bodies to the outside, and building the potential for a male body with more red blood cells and a stronger bone structure. This is, in fact, a hunter's body, for our brain structure is still very like the brains of early hunter/gatherers. This change of focus has the effect of leaving boys behind in the brain-growing race, and particularly in the development of the slower growing left hemisphere.

The newborn brain

When babies are born, they have a hundred thousand million brain cells, each capable of linking with 20,000 other cells. This enormous number of cells has some hard-wired links to ensure survival, such as breathing, sucking and crying. However every child's newborn brain also has other hard-wired links related to the chances of their unborn life – music and voices, sensitivity to foods and flavours, and randomly generated links. These are described in an essay by Steven Pinker as '...chance events in the development of the brain in utero, such as whether some neurons zigged or zagged at a particular day in brain development'. 'The Blank Slate: The Modern Denial of Human Nature' (Harvard 2005)

Boys will have made more links in the more developed right hemisphere of their brain, girls may have even crossed the corpus callosum, the super-highway linking the right brain and the left brain, and be using both sides of their brain in unison.

At birth, babies' brains are smooth and almost flat; it is the linking synapses between brain cells that eventually force their brains to crumple up into the more familiar 'walnut' shape we are familiar with in adult brains, just so they can fit in their skulls. The grey matter (made up of closely packed brain cells) tends to cluster near the skull; the white matter (all the synapses linking the cells) fills the space within the brain, working like a huge telephone exchange sending messages throughout the brain and between the hemispheres.

Functions and features of the brain

It would be a mistake not to look at some relevant functions and features of the brain before exploring the stories of eight boys, but it is not our intention to provide readers with a detailed discourse on the structure of the brain, just an overview of the key features which affect early learning, and particularly the learning of boys.

When you look at the brain from above it is formed in two definite halves or **hemispheres**, and in adults the halves have roughly the same size and complexity. Of course, you can't see this without a brain scan, but in children the brain is much more lopsided, with the right side of the brain much more developed and connected than the left, and in most boys, even more so. The right side of the brain handles movement, particularly gross motor, whole body movement. It also processes imagination, dreams, music, expressive language, emotion and what has been called the 'big picture' of generality and knowledge clumped together.

The left side of the brain, developing later in all children, and particularly in boys, majors in detail. The centres that direct and process fine motor control, order, sequence, letters and words reside in this hemisphere, and in order to make sense of these, and begin the complex tasks of reading and writing, children need to work in both sides of their brains simultaneously, connecting the hemispheres by using the thick band of the corpus callosum which joins them. Some girls will have been using the corpus callosum since before birth, and this is why they are generally ready to read and use fine motor skills before most boys. To recap:

- The left side of the brain develops more slowly in boys and the necessary links between the hemispheres to facilitate reading often don't develop until boys are between six and eight.
- Boys' enthusiasm for active learning is directly linked to their thinking in the right brain. Fine motor control develops later and can only build on and *follow* gross motor development.
- In early childhood, many girls will be using language centres in both sides of their brains. Most boys will still be processing language in the right hemisphere, making it difficult for them to separate talking and moving.

When you look at the brain from the back of the head, it is divided into four sections, each with a definite history and function! Working from the bottom, there is the **brain stem**, also called the primitive brain, which is crucial in nerve communication with the rest of the body. It also controls essential functions like breathing and blinking, which we do automatically. It is not logical, its responses are simple reflexes, particularly to stress, and under stress these reflexes can send us deep into our primitive brains where we choose a response – 'fight, flight or freeze'. Being able to control these primitive responses is what makes us human, and it isn't easy, particularly when testosterone is making the brain agitated. To complicate matters, the mechanism for managing reflex response is located in the next part of the brain.

Sitting round the top of the brain stem like a collar is the **limbic system**, consisting of the **cerebellum** and the **amygdala**, which is sometimes called the mammalian brain, linking us to cats, dogs, apes and dolphins. This part of the brain contains the long-term memory processor, coordinates our physical actions, and plays a key role in emotional stability and health. The amygdala (sometimes called the 'gatekeeper') is a vital part of the limbic system, because it stops us moving into the primitive brain and simplistic responses when we are under stress. So:

- Control of the limbic system and the amygdala develops more slowly in boys, and this means they have less control over the gatekeeper. They are more likely to respond to stress with 'fight, flight or freeze', and much more likely than most girls to strike out when cortisol levels are raised in their brains in response to pressure to sit still, to change activities too quickly, to focus on too many things or to process emotions or complicated instructions.
- The development of impulse control is slow. Most young boys need help and time to process new information and situations, or they will respond through their primitive brains.

Control of the amygdala is activated by the newest part of the human brain, sometimes called the **neo-cortex**. This is the crumpled outer covering of the brain, and the most sophisticated, processing thought, reasoning, sensory input, language, emotions and decision-making. It also the slowest part to develop in humans, and is not fully functioning until late in childhood. The sections of the cortex have different roles and develop at different times, generally from the back of the head to the front, where the most important **pre-frontal lobes** are situated. These lobes are crucial in problem solving, decision-making, attention and control of impulse. The pre-frontal lobes are also involved in higher order thinking skills and concepts such as compassion, altruism and justice. Remember that:

- Development of the neo-cortex will be slower in some boys, who have not completed its construction until adolescence, or even later. Boys need more time to think, to reason and to process. Stress and pressure may force them to leave the cortex and descend past the amygdala into the primitive brain, where instinct rather than reason will control their responses.

There are significant differences between the structure and growth of the brains of boys and girls, but there are many more similarities than differences, and these are inexorably tied up with genetic make-up, nurture and chance. However, we should not think that we must wait for the brain to mature in its own time, sitting around watching for maturity to emerge. Parents, practitioners and teachers (to say nothing of society as a whole) have a responsibility to support and enable the healthy growth of children's bodies and their brains. Research has now clearly demonstrated the influence on brain building of such factors as diet, secure attachment, parental model, screen time (both TV and computers), peer and media pressure and family circumstances. We would do well to heed these messages.

The optimum conditions for children

Balance is all, and we should provide the optimum conditions for children where they feel confident, valued and securely attached. If we want children to become self-regulating, responsive and creative thinkers, with a sense of community and loyalty, some of the best ways to do this are to:

1 recognise the unique nature of every child, every boy and every girl;
2 understand that although boys' and girls' brains develop in similar ways, there are significant differences, and we ignore them at our peril;
3 make learning enjoyable, not stressful, because calming endorphins in the body will help the brain to learn;
4 reduce stress by watching and listening carefully to the messages from children, picking up on the signals they are giving you, so you can work out the best way to help;
5 work together, using the strengths, knowledge and commitment of parents, practitioners, teachers and others;
6 follow the lives of the boys in your care with the interest that is demonstrated by the adults in this book;
7 remember that love, compassion, clear boundaries and high expectations are the best tools for combating the difficulties that children face;
8 make no assumptions.

Eight principles to guide you; eight boys in this book – they are eight of the thousands that will pass our way. Some will have characteristics that you recognise, and some will be facing the same life chances. Not all the strategies will be relevant to the boys you know, but we offer you their stories and the ways the adults helped them to cope with the magical and random mix of nature, nurture, culture and chance of their lives. We hope this will help you to understand the boys in your lives.

The Cleverness of Boys

Paul the risk taker

Paul's story

There wasn't much that could reduce little Paul Clamp to tears, but what happened that day nearly had me wailing as well, not so much in sympathy but in sheer, abject frustration! Had I not been crystal clear about *which* trees could be climbed and which were most definitely off limits? Had I not been extra vigilant in my supervision of this lively bunch of children? Either way, as I entreated the distraught, howling Paul to keep still I decided that now was not at all the time to consider such profound questions!

'I'm gunna fall,' he screamed as I did my best to keep him calm. I was tempted to tell him that fall was the very last thing he could do, but giving vent to my own emotions would probably only inflame an already difficult situation. There was no doubt about it, his knee was not going to budge. It was wedged in the fork of a sturdy branch as sure as if it had been concreted there! I was just grateful that my colleagues were so supportive. My teaching assistant Pam had gone for help while some very nice teachers from another school minded my class as well as their own.

A trip to the Botanical Gardens and City Farm with my reception class had seemed such a good idea at the time but now I began to wonder whether it had been naïve to assume that Paul could have survived it without some sort of minor catastrophe blighting the day.

He continued to sob inconsolably as the other children looked on with disbelief.

'Will he have to stay there all night?' asked Kev.

'Will the fire brigade come?' asked Daniel enthusiastically.

'Will they have to cut off 'is leg?' enquired another, not at all helpfully as this only caused the usually heroic Paul to wail all the louder. It didn't usually matter how hard he fell or what he bumped into, tears were not something Paul usually concerned himself with. However, today was decidedly different and as he saw Pam approaching followed by two large men with a ladder, the sobbing turned into terrified screaming.

One of the men was young and agile and when Paul saw him climb effortlessly into the tree the sobbing gave way to interested admiration. Paul was fond of telling us that he was the 'besttest climber out of everybody,' but this was climbing as he'd never quite seen it before. He gazed in astonishment as the young man leapt on to the branch that was trapping the leg and then swung ape-like to the end of the branch. As he did this, the older of the two men climbed up the ladder with a brick in his hand and as the young man's weight forced the branch down, he wedged the brick underneath Paul's leg.

'That should do the trick!' he said, hopefully, then slowly and carefully he began to pull the now smiling Paul from the tree. He tried to bring Paul down the ladder, but the now miraculously recovered child was having nothing of it. 'I can do it myself,' he shouted emphatically, and in the next minute he had scrambled down from the tree to the cheers of the other children. Looking relatively unscathed, he was obviously enjoying the attention! As for me, although my nerves were in tatters I didn't have the heart to remonstrate with him. That could wait until tomorrow!

The next day I went to work resolved to have a firm word with Paul about the wisdom of thinking things through before launching into action, but it was just 'one of those mornings' and by the time lunchtime arrived there hadn't been a moment to spare. It would just have to wait until the afternoon. Over lunchtime, various staff began to share their experiences of time spent with the adventurous Paul. Apparently, on a recent trip to the park with his mum and dad he had hurled himself into the paddling pool to retrieve his football. His parents, who had been busy collecting pine cones with his little sister, had been horrified when they looked up and saw a pile of clothes on the grass and Paul in the middle of the pool completely naked!

He just seemed one of those little boys who saw no fear in anything. When he and his friends had built the tower as high as they could reach he was always the one who would find some way of accessing sundry pieces of furniture that could be precariously balanced on while further pieces were added. He was the first to volunteer to hold the snake when the animal man came, and no-one could accuse him of not making the most of our recently developed outdoor area.

He loved nothing more than to ride in, or push others in wheeled toys at high speed, and he showed a considerable talent for risk assessment. It was rare for him or any of his playmates to be hurt. His favourite pursuit was climbing. He was the fastest to the top of the climbing frame and enjoyed nothing more, when we got the use of the school hall, than shinning to the top of the ropes. So why, I ask myself, should I have been surprised when a somewhat flustered lunchtime supervisor arrived to announce that Paul was on the roof?

This simply couldn't be true! Not after yesterday, surely not! But as I arrived in the outside area I could see that it definitely was true! There, on top of the flat roof stood a triumphant Paul holding the muddy ball he had just fished out of the guttering.

'Don't move,' I shouted with authority. 'Stay exactly where you are and we'll get the site manager to come and get you down.'

'But I can get down by myself,' protested Paul, who, after throwing the ball to one of his mates proceeded to slide down the drainpipe. It was too late to stop him, and fortunately, the roof was not high so I was able to grab him by the backside and at least offer some protection against him falling, which actually would have been very unlikely as he rarely exceeded what he knew to be his own limitations. Nevertheless, I now felt an even greater urgency to talk to him about the incident the previous day! So, the said conversation took place that very afternoon and concluded with Paul promising to 'fink carefully' before climbing again.

The next few weeks passed relatively uneventfully and anyway, with an impending Ofsted inspection I was somewhat preoccupied! It wasn't until the middle of the inspection that Paul distinguished himself again. His first faux pas involved a somewhat elderly lay inspector. While she was examining the displays by the creative area he asked her whether she was going to die soon! When she told him that she very much hoped not, he affirmed that he was sure that she would. She kindly asked him to explain. 'Well,' he announced, 'my Nan's hair went white like yours and then she died!' Before the bemused inspector could respond he was off to the 'finding out' area to see if he could find something to disassemble. After climbing, disassembling things was probably his favourite activity.

Paul shrieked with delight when he saw the riches of the finding out area. One of the cleaners had donated an old-fashioned cylinder vacuum cleaner that no longer worked. 'Wow,' shrieked Paul, grabbing a screwdriver, 'look at this!' For the next half an hour he was deeply engrossed in taking the thing to pieces. He stopped periodically to ask someone a question, or show off a component he had removed from the cleaner, and his concentration would probably have remained unbroken had it not been for the lead inspector who approached the table and stood over him watching what he was doing. Now, I don't think this man was much accustomed to talking to very young children, because if he had been, he probably wouldn't have said what he did! He spoke very kindly, if a little patronisingly, as he pointed to the vacuum cleaner and enquired of Paul, 'Is that a space rocket?'

Paul looked amazed that anyone could think this. 'No mate,' he announced, obviously unaware of the importance of our visitor, 'this here is a vacuum cleaner!' He then proceeded to laugh uncontrollably as the inspector retreated from the room.

It has to be said that life with Paul around was never dull. Paul was always going to be one of those boys you would never forget, and some years later I was to bump into Paul once again, in what at first seemed the most surprising way, although, if I think about it, it actually made perfect sense.

I had recently moved into an old Victorian house in need of a considerable amount of work. In fact, there was such a lot to do that I'm afraid the slipped tiles on the roof had been somewhat ignored. It was not until there was a series of bad storms that getting them fixed became an imperative. As I didn't know any roofers it seemed sensible just to pick up the Yellow Pages and follow my intuition. An appointment was made and a middle aged gentleman turned up to assess the work and give me an estimate.

Not long after this, as the weather took a turn for the better, my anxiety about the slipped tiles subsided and I almost forgot about the work on the roof. It was not until I heard a prolonged ring on the doorbell that I twigged it was the day for the roof repairs to begin. I hastened to the door and as I opened it, was completely unprepared for the sight that met my eyes. There on the front doorstep, with a wide smile on his face, stood a grown-up Paul Clamp!

Obviously he still enjoyed climbing and had turned his first love into a full-time career. At first he didn't recognise me, but even though a good few years had elapsed, I'd have known that face anywhere. Mind you, this time it was my intention to simply let him get on with the job. I certainly wasn't going to stand underneath waiting to catch him this time! All I can say is, the extensive climbing practice in his early years had obviously paid off. He never slipped once and did an excellent job of mending my roof!

How Paul's brain affects his behaviour

What is going on in Paul's brain as he takes risks in behaviour, language and relationships? How do we learn to see these characteristics and behaviours as 'clevernesses', rather than feeling irritation and seeing the possible dangers to Paul and others? How does Paul's behaviour in the reception class demonstrate the tension between nature, nurture, culture and chance? Recognising his real strengths and helping him to manage his risk-taking nature needs understanding and flexibility from his parents, the practitioners and teachers who work with him, and Paul himself.

As we discuss Paul and the other boys in this book, looking at the reasons for their behaviour and learning styles, we need to acknowledge new research into the differences between the brains and bodies of boys and girls. Less than

50 years ago, most people believed that gender differences were entirely the result of nurture (the upbringing of individuals and their families) and culture (the expectations of society at the time). These two influences were thought to be the major influences, with little acceptance that nature (what we are born with, our genetic code) or chance had much influence at all.

We now know without doubt, particularly from evidence provided by CAT and MRI scans, that nature not only makes a significant contribution to our gender balance, but that it may well be the most influential of all – more than the way we are brought up or what society expects of us. From the instant of conception, the genetic blueprint of each unique child predisposes some behaviours and will reduce or eliminate others. As we have discussed in the introductory chapters of this book, gender is a point on a spectrum, which is first established at conception, reinforced in the womb by repeated floods of human chemicals, then, and only then, affected by the outside world of family and society, with its life chances.

In previous decades boys like Paul, and the other characters in this book, spent most of their young childhood out-of-doors. They would have been out of the sight of adults, learning in an active, hands-on way with their friends. They used their wits and competed against their own bodies and those of their group or gang. I was the middle child of five siblings, and climbing trees, jumping ditches, lighting fires and making camps with my three brothers were daily occupations for us all, with my sister and I trailing behind and trying to keep up. Winter and summer, we went outside after breakfast (and sometimes before) and were still outside as it got dark and our mother called us in saying, 'I thought I said come in when it was dark!'. We lived an outdoor life, with the risks and excitements that that entailed.

Paul's brain is an outdoor brain, the brain of a hunter, quick-witted, highly focused and competitive, naturally tuned to taking risks and trying things out. It's not just the opportunities he has, or the models from television and local culture. His genetic make-up and the physical growth and architecture of his brain cannot be denied. However, his life is very different from generations before him, perhaps more different than we might think, and his behaviour is constrained in so many ways. He is not able to spend as much of his time out-of-doors, despite the understanding of the adults who work with him. He is much more supervised, our safety-conscious society allows less risk, and there are fewer opportunities to test his strength and skills. The trees, rocks and streams where his parents and grandparents played have been replaced by carefully designed climbing apparatus in purpose built playgrounds where risk has been so reduced that Paul's instincts are often denied.

Key elements of the brain

Let's look more closely at some of the key elements of Paul's brain and how they are developing into a unique structure, formed by nature (the biology and genetics), by nurture (how the child is brought up by his family and other carers) and chance (the assumptions and responses of society from the moment of his birth, and the accidents and opportunities he will encounter on the way). Each of these elements has an effect on the child, but in the last decade, we have established without doubt that nature plays such an important part that the nature/nurture debate is now clearly favouring nature.

What has already happened before birth is so important that we can no longer say that gender is a 'plastic' element, easily moulded by nurture to create adult gender disposition. We know for sure that from the first day of life, every baby has a clearly established gender disposition that will play a strong part in what they will become. Foetal testosterone, flooding the womb in pregnancy triggers the development of each boy and identifies their unique place on the gender spectrum, which stretches from the most masculine position to the most feminine. This is the first building block of gender for each child and the starting point for their life as a boy or a girl.

The structure of human bodies and brains has not changed much since we were living in caves. Males are still built to hunt and females to nurture, and risk-taking is part of the nature of a hunter. Recent research has identified more than 100 differences between the brains of males and those of females, and among these is that boys' naturally have more dopamine in their blood streams, and dopamine is a chemical that increases risk-taking. Add to this the natural tendency of boys to be 'doing' which results from a more muscular body and a higher number of red blood cells, and the urge to climb high, run fast, keep up with the chase is understandable. No amount of debate or discussion will change Paul's instincts.

Paul's position on the gender spectrum is towards the extreme male end, with strong features of human maleness – strength, tenacity, single-mindedness, and a tendency to take risks and enjoy a sense of danger. If we could use a PET or MRI scan to see how his brain affects his body and behaviour, we would probably see the following features, which may well result in tensions between Paul's strengths (his 'clevernesses') and the demands that early education is making on him:

- Because Paul's body produces more dopamine than girls and many other boys, Paul is an impulsive risk-taker, rarely thinking about what he does before he does it, and usually getting away without damaging himself or others. This makes him take the opportunities that life offers, and can be seen as a real advantage or a real problem, depending on who you are!

- If we ask his mother, she will say Paul was a big, heavy baby, his genetic make-up, his bone structure and his muscle bulk made him so. Different boys, at different places on the gender spectrum, will have had different birth weights, differently affected by foetal testosterone. Paul's position in the continuum is towards the heavier, more muscular end, and he will be among the tallest and strongest boys in his group, striving always to be the most competitive runner and racer, the best 'mover and shaper' in large construction, and the model of risk-taking for his peers. His natural energy and physical strength make it difficult for him to conform to many of the expectations of the current education system, which often brings him into conflict with adults.

- Because he is at the extreme of the 'hunter' continuum of boys, Paul is also more active and restless than many other boys. Testosterone will probably have resulted in more red blood cells, which, with his muscular body give him both strength and stamina, perfect for a hunter. They will also make him more fidgety when he is asked to sit still. His parents and practitioners observe that he is constantly on the move, and even when he is concentrating on quiet activities, his body is still moving. Muscle bulk and strength of this sort will also make Paul more competitive. Testosterone binds a pack of boys, it also makes them compete for leadership. Without the hunt, Paul and boys like him will often engage in physical rough and tumble which is intended to exercise essential muscles and establish a 'pecking order' in the pack.

- The amygdala is an almond-shaped organ deep in the brain that controls our impulses. In all boys, the amygdala is bigger, but in many boys it develops its controlling role later than in girls. This means that Paul is less able than most girls and some other boys to control his impulse to act or to speak, particularly when he is under pressure. In Paul's story, climbing forbidden trees and speaking his mind are examples of his impulsivity. Impulsivity may also get him into trouble for 'smart remarks' and thoughtless comments.

- Sitting still and listening are not Paul's strengths, and in school he often has to stop doing activities he enjoys in order to follow the school programme. The teachers we experience are chance factors in our lives, and Paul's teacher is patient, giving him as much time as she can when these transitions are necessary. Pressure to do too many things at once, or to stop quickly when he is involved in an activity will lead to the production of cortisol and adrenalin (stress hormones) resulting in frustration and anger – and behaviour management issues for everyone.

- Like most boys, Paul's listening and memory are slow to develop. His hippocampus (which helps his memory) will develop more slowly than the same brain area in a girl, or even in some boys. His temporal lobes, with their role in memory and listening, are finding it difficult to both hear and remember the instructions and warnings of his parents and the practitioners in the school. He finds it hard to interpret voices when people are speaking to him. He absorbs less information from the unspoken messages given by facial expression, body language and voice tone, and he picks up less of what is going on, particularly if the information is in words.

- The corpus callosum (the superhighway linking the two halves of the brain) is smaller in boys, and carries fewer connections between left and right hemispheres. This feature is both a strength and a weakness. It is a weakness because Paul finds it much harder than other children to do more than one thing at a time, often referred to as 'multitasking'. As we now know, most females are much better at this, and some women feel multitasking is a greater advantage than single focus. However, a strength for Paul is that single focus is something he is very good at. His parents and the practitioners at the nursery will comment on how difficult it is to distract him from something he is really involved in, such as dismantling the vacuum cleaner.

Left to his own devices in a free, self-chosen day, Paul would probably excel. He would take the chances each day offered to explore, invent, and test his skills of climbing, jumping, bike riding and other physical skills. He would make dens, swings and carts, and in the 1960s and 1970s there would have been a Paul on every street, in every park and garden. He would have been the envy of all the local boys, although adults may have felt much the same about his behaviour as his teacher does now. He may have been described as 'wild' or 'a bad influence'.

Other influences

At home, nurture and culture reinforce Paul's 'clevernesses'. His Mum and Dad both work, but they arrange bike rides, visits to adventure parks and walks in all weathers during the weekends and holidays. His uncle plays football for the local team and gave Paul a football for his second birthday, teaching him how to use it in endless games at the local park.

Of course, our culture recognises and rewards physical skill and risk-taking. Radio, TV and other media are full of the exploits of boys and men like Paul. He watches sport and other risk-taking activities regularly on TV, reinforcing the image of the risk-taker as someone to admire and emulate. Sporting stars are constantly in the news for their exploits, and the current media interest in 'taking things to the limit' whether in driving, sport or in reconstructing schoolboy scientific experiments, reinforces this risk-taking mentality. Paul, his dad and his uncle will often watch these programmes together, laughing, shoving each other, falling about, and making other low-level physical contact as they delight in these public exhibitions of testosterone at work.

Before he went on to a full time place in an early years unit, Paul benefited from pre-school provision with an understanding childminder, who has a big garden and plenty of patience. The chance of nurture in this setting reinforced Paul's natural skills. Paul currently returns to her in the school breaks and holidays and she is very good at harnessing his energy in physical activities and plenty of outdoor play.

However, for most of the time Paul is at school. Like all children in the UK he started school before his fifth birthday, and like others, he now has to spend large parts of his day doing things he hasn't chosen, often in an indoor environment. Whenever he is free to go out, he does, and most of the activities and objects that interest him are outside.

Being indoors is frustrating and difficult for him, his physical bulk means he is often seen as restless and clumsy, and the activities on offer indoors, with their emphasis on reading, writing and fine-motor skills present a combination of challenge and irrelevance to him. His teacher's addition of a 'finding out and dismantling table' is an inspiration and he spends time there voluntarily, sometimes referring to the books she has displayed nearby, sometimes taking photos of the stages of dismantling. His involvement in most other indoor or sedentary activities is reluctant and grudging. He fidgets and moves around constantly as he completes them.

How to recognise and value the strengths of boys like Paul

So what are Paul's 'clevernesses' and what can we learn from his experience? How can we recognise and value these 'clevernesses' in the boys like Paul in our own settings and families? If we are going to help these boys, should we try to change the boys or change the way we provide for them? Michael Gurian in *The Minds of Boys* (Jossey Bass 2005) says that the problem is not an organisational one, not an issue of teaching style, but a moral one. Are we morally justified in 'corralling boys into an educational culture, which risks damaging their self-image and motivation for the long term' – and if so, what should conscientious practitioners do to maintain their professional obligations while meeting the needs of every child?

Paul is clever at risk-taking, single-focus active learning and physical skills. How can we build a curriculum for him that involves, interests and motivates him, and through these, provides him with the skills he needs to manage his learning in the future? The skills of communication, reading, writing and calculating are all essential to a full life, whether that is as a roofer or a researcher, but so are the qualities of courage, problem-solving and concentration.

One of the challenges to everyone who works with boys like Paul is to balance their enthusiasm and joy in activity and risk while ensuring that their sense of self-worth and pride in their growing skills is maintained. The current pressures in schools to reach targets in reading and writing can be a problem both for Paul and the adults who live and work with him.

When Paul started at nursery, the practitioners discussed his needs, and worked with his parents to support his interest in and lively approach to life. His father was (and still is) proud of Paul's physical skills and adventurous nature, and was concerned that he should not be discouraged from the activities they both loved. He did admit that Paul's adventures, and the scrapes he got into as a result, were becoming legendary in the neighbourhood and recognised that a successful adult life needed a balance of risk and security.

Here are some of the strategies that seemed to help Paul during his time in the early years:

- Boys like Paul need to learn how to manage their own impulsivity and risky behaviour. They need to pause, think, concentrate and remember about safe behaviour and control of their impulses. This will inevitably take time to learn, and for many boys, control of impulsive behaviour may not be achieved until they are in their twenties, or even beyond. In the meantime, these strategies did help Paul in his early years and may help boys like him, and his teachers recommend them to you:

- Reward appropriate risk-taking and physical activity by talking about it, giving verbal and physical praise (a hug, pat on the back and so on). Risk-taking is often openly or secretly admired by other children, while attracting disapproval from adults, so catch them doing things you can approve of, by spending time outside, observing them in free choice play and offering them 'safe risk'.
- Give boys plenty of activities that involve shifting, building, lifting, carrying, dismantling and constructing, particularly outside. Provide tyres, big bricks, planks, ladders, wheelbarrows, trucks, and heavy things to lift, move and rearrange. Photograph their experiments and constructions, talk about them in group sessions, and display the photos where parents and other children can see and appreciate them. Praise effort and new ways of doing things, and build them into everyday experiences and tasks – don't just say, 'I need a strong boy to help move this table!'
- Think about Paul and boys like him when you are planning small group tasks and problem-solving activities. Spend some of your group time outside where they will be more relaxed, and use the materials and equipment they enjoy. Given a bit of thought and an open mind, mathematical, scientific and language challenges, as well as more formal teaching can often be adapted to incorporate large motor skills and outdoor apparatus.
- Our example child has now grown up to be a successful adult, involved in a risk-taking, physical job which suits his skills. Make sure you offer examples of active adult occupations, not just the more sedentary professions. Try to get a scaffolder, firefighter or other person who does an active job to come and talk about their work, explaining and describing both the excitement and the dangers!

- Paul finds listening, concentration and remembering harder than some other children, and particularly most girls, so:
  - Speak clearly, and remember that he may have difficulty interpreting the tone of your voice. Repeat instructions and teach him to 'self-talk', repeating the instruction or reminder three times to himself in a whisper, or in his head to reinforce the message. Make sentences short, and use fewer words than you think you might need!

- Encourage him to look at you while you give explanations and instructions. Boys often find eye contact difficult and need to be reminded to look at the person who is speaking, and rewarded when they do. Boys who spend a lot of time watching TV and computer screens may find it even harder, so persevere with understanding, as these boys may find maintaining eye contact with you very stressful.

- Paul is very good at focusing on one thing at a time, and gets more involved in activities than many other children:
  - Give him plenty of time for activities he is interested in. Many boys like Paul can concentrate for up to an hour (or even more) on an activity that captures their interest. Try to make child-initiated activity time as long as possible, and offer this early in the day, so energetic boys have time to follow their interests before you ask them to sit and listen.
  - It is now evident that engagement in large motor activity just before a spell of fine motor activity is particularly helpful for boys like Paul, so if you are going to embark on a concentrated activity that he has found difficult in the past, make sure he has had some physical activity just before you start – try vigorous action songs, a simple 'brain break' activity or physical activities as a group.
  - Give time and early warning of the end of activity periods, so these boys have 'transition time' – time to bring their activities to a comfortable end. This will reduce stress and frustration.

With the help of his parents and the understanding of his teachers, Paul is now successful in maximising his continuing desire for risk in a valued and valuable job in his community. The chance meeting with a friend of his uncle opened the way to training in roofing techniques. His own boy, now three years old, may be in your group!

The Cleverness of Boys

Adam the scientist

Adam's story

It's not unusual for people working with young children to look drained at the end of a hard day, but today, my colleague Maureen was looking more than usually exhausted. As I walked into the empty classroom she was propped against a wall looking every bit as if she was frozen there!

'Are you OK?' I enquired with some concern.

Coming to with a shake of her head she replied. 'Me! Oh I'm fine. It's just been one of those days, and Adam has *really* been on form today!'

'Why, what's he been up to now?' I asked with interest.

I should explain that Adam was one of those little boys who could move at the speed of light, and because of his poor eyesight and dubious coordination would bowl over anything that stood in his path, oblivious to the trail of devastation he left behind him! Mind you, it didn't help that he had a strong aversion to his glasses. Consequently, his first task of the day was to hide them somewhere where no-one could find them and by the end of the morning, even he couldn't remember where he'd put them!

Maureen slumped into a chair and began to explain. 'Well,' she said, 'it started in the book corner. I was just about to add some new books to the author display when I noticed Adam sitting in the middle of the carpet surrounded by lots of bits and pieces, which I realised to my horror, were pieces of Jan Pienkowski's *Haunted House* book!' (Most early years practitioners will be familiar with this excellent pop-up book.)

Maureen continued, 'Anyway, Adam was completely engrossed in the task of systematically disassembling the book. I tried not to be cross, although it wasn't easy as several of the other children had made a special request for it at storytime, and it wasn't going to be possible now.' Maureen pointed to a sorry pile of pieces of card on the table beside her, as I stifled a smile of amusement.

She went on to explain, 'So I stayed very calm and asked Adam what he was doing. He looked at me over his glasses, which for once he was wearing, and informed me that he was finding out how it worked! When I looked a little shocked he confidently informed me that he was going to put it back together again, but as you can see, this proved to be beyond him!' At this point we both began howling with laughter.

Once we had recovered, Maureen went on to recount Adam's *piece de resistance* for that day.

'And then, when it came to home time, Adam was nowhere to be seen. I went off to search for him and finally found him in the toilets huddled over the wash basin. He had obviously decided to skip tidy-up time, and there he was, in deep concentration, stirring something in a small bucket from the sand area. When I asked him what he was doing he looked at me mysteriously and told me he was making a potion. Feeling a little guilty for being somewhat abrupt, I asked him how he made it.'

'I made it out of hot water and soap,' he replied enthusiastically. 'It's a magic potion...you try some!'

Maureen explained that she hadn't the heart to refuse and continued with the story. 'I looked at the thick slimy potion in the bucket and pretended to have a drink. Whereupon Adam pointed a finger at me and informed me that now I must die!' I asked him why.

'Because it's poison!' he announced triumphantly.

'So did you die?' I enquired with interest.

'Oh yes,' she said, 'I died there and then on the toilet floor and played dead until Adam leaned over me and told me I could get up!'

'Maureen,' I said with a grimace, 'you don't know what you might catch from the toilet floor!'

'I know,' she said the things we do for kids!' We both laughed again.

As I left Maureen to carry on with her preparations for the following day, I smiled to myself, blissfully unaware that I would soon find myself embroiled in one of Adam's intriguing lines of enquiry.

The next day dawned bright and sunny. All the doors were open and most of the children were outside. Adam and some of his friends were in the digging area in shorts, t-shirts and wellie boots, which mostly didn't match and were mostly on the wrong feet. (But at least they had done it by themselves!) In spite of the heat they were digging with great energy.

'Look, there's another 'un!' announced Adam throwing a stone on to a small pile of similar stones that lay nearby. This was too much for me. I had to go and find out what was *so* capturing their interest.

As I walked towards the digging area I was spotted by Adam who beckoned me excitedly towards a pile of beautifully smooth, egg-shaped stones. 'Look Mrs Bayley, look! We found a whole load of dinosaur eggs and we're going to hatch 'em all ain't we John!'

'Yeah, we are,' explained John. 'We're gunna wrap 'em up and make 'em warm until the little baby dinosaurs come out!'

I looked at the stones. They were about the size of a quail's egg and I had to confess, perfectly egg shaped. 'So what will you wrap them in and where will you keep them?' I asked with interest.

'We're going to wrap 'em in paper towels and put 'em on the radiator,' said John.

'Don't be stupid,' replied Adam, 'the radiators ain't on in the summer. We'll have to put 'em on the windowsill in the sunshine.'

'Perhaps we could find a box and some warm cotton wool and straw to put them in,' I suggested.

The boys seemed to like this idea so I proposed that someone should come with me to search for materials. 'You go John,' said Adam, 'and I'll stay here and finish digging to see if there's any more eggs down here.'

'OK' shrieked John, as he ran towards the door. 'Let's go to the workshop area, we should find a good box there and then we can get some of the rabbit's straw. Where we gunna get cotton wool from Mrs Bayley?'

'I think there's some in the creative area,' I replied, trying to keep up with him.

John dashed round like a whirlwind and it wasn't long before he'd collected everything he thought we might need. Finally, he stood still for a moment, thinking. 'D'you think we'd better wash the eggs before we put 'em in the box, 'cause there's loads of dirt on 'em?'

'It might be a good idea,' I said, and before I could say anything else John was off to get the eggs.

'Don't drop 'em!' implored Adam, and in a flash they were inside filling the sink with warm water.

'Oh, look at 'em Miss, they've gone all shiny!' exclaimed an excited Adam as he washed the eggs with great care. Meanwhile John prepared the box for its precious bounty. The eggs were then dried with paper towels and thoughtfully placed into the box. If they had been made of gold and encrusted with diamonds they could not have been treated with greater respect!

'Now we've got to make a sign what says DON'T TOUCH,' announced Adam. More frantic activity followed as materials were collected for the sign, and then the box was placed on the windowsill with great ceremony. Adam stood back and admired his work. 'I wonder if they'll have hatched by tomorrow. I bet when we come in the morning there'll be little baby dinosaurs all over the classroom!'

'Yeah,' said John, 'there'll most probably be Triceratops and Stegosaurus and Apatosaurus un all!'

'I can't wait,' said Adam, literally shaking with excitement. I noticed he wasn't wearing his glasses which meant another mammoth hunt at the end of the morning!

For the rest of the day the boys engaged in a range of their favourite activities, but I saw with interest that Adam kept returning to the box where he would stand and stare at the eggs for prolonged periods of time. I didn't like to interrupt him but imagined that he was thinking about what might emerge from his precious find.

As I opened up the doors the next morning Adam came flying up the path followed by his somewhat harassed and long-suffering mother who was pushing his younger brother in a pushchair. To be honest, I had forgotten about the eggs until I saw him. He ran towards me shouting.

'Have they hatched yet Mrs Bayley?'

'Oh, Adam, I don't know,' I replied truthfully, 'we'd better go and look.'

Adam shot across the room to look into the box and the look of disappointment on his face when he saw the stones lying there exactly where he had left them the previous day would have moved even the hardest heart.

'Oh look,' he said, 'there's nothing there!'

I tried to be reassuring. 'Well they'll probably take a bit longer than one day you know!'

Adam smiled. 'Yes, I bet that's it,' he said, 'they just need a bit longer.' For the rest of the day Adam was uncharacteristically quiet. He didn't even bother to try and hide his glasses and wasn't interested in the battery-operated robot that James Robinson had bought in. Such things would normally have him jumping up and down with excitement. This morning, he just kept staring at the eggs, then halfway through the morning he came to see me, face beaming.

'I've got it miss,' he announced, 'we ain't keeping 'em warm enough, we need one of them things like what my uncle keeps his plants in!' It didn't take me long to work out that he was referring to a propagator, and as luck would have it I had one at home.

'I've got one of those at home Adam,' I said, 'I could bring it tomorrow if you like.'

'Oh thanks Mrs Bayley,' said Adam, who by now was looking much more cheerful. That should make 'em hatch shouldn't it!' That night I sorted out the propagator and put it in the car ready to take to school the next day, and just as I expected, Adam was there bright and early and we were soon setting up the propagator and transferring the eggs to their new home.

Throughout the morning Adam returned at frequent intervals to check for progress and was ecstatic when he picked up the eggs and found they were warm. 'I think they'll hatch soon now,' he said with confidence.

As time went on Maureen and I wondered about the wisdom of what was happening. Should we have told Adam that they were only stones and that there was no possible chance that they would hatch? Were we right to let him follow his own line of enquiry and face the inevitable disappointment? Were we deceiving him and was this carrying learning through discovery too far? However, after several days of heart searching and much inspection of the eggs by Adam, it was Adam himself who resolved the matter.

It must have been about two o'clock in the afternoon when he approached me. He was carrying his box with extreme care and he had a serious look on his face.

'Where are you taking your eggs Adam?' I asked with genuine interest.

'Outside to the digging area,' he replied. Then after a pause he looked at me and said, 'I think they were buried for too long and that they's probably all dead on the inside.' With that, he carried them outside and tenderly and lovingly reburied them.

How Adam's brain affects his behaviour

Adam and his friends are present in every group of children. We may say to ourselves 'I wonder what will become of all this experiment as these boys grow up? Will it result in new scientific findings on the edge of human thinking? Or will it become the mindless vandalism that we see in our streets and parks, where boys (and even sometimes girls) seem to take delight in destroying the efforts of others? Do boys really need to test things to destruction?'

The answer is probably 'Yes', but we do not need to stand back and despair, and let culture or chance lead these boys into the street behaviour where gangs and destruction become mindless declarations of independence. Despite all the evidence to the contrary, boys really do have *more* need for order and rules, and to know who is boss. Testosterone in their bodies and brains means they need to move, but they also need to know who is in charge. They are constantly testing us, and their friends, to establish the rules and find the boundaries. Boys feel insecure when they don't know who is making the rules, and their response will often be to become *more* extreme as they continue to test where the limits are.

In his book *Raising Boys* (Thorsons 2003), Steve Biddulph says: 'If no-one is in charge, they begin jostling with each other to establish a pecking order. Their testosterone driven make-up leads them to want to set up hierarchies, but they can't always do it because they are all the same age. If we provide structure, then they can relax'. In Adam's setting, the adults are clear about rules, and the children feel safe within them. The boys know that their interests will be supported and their enthusiasm will be encouraged, so when they get obsessed with dinosaur eggs, the adults will help them to explore.

Key elements of the brain

Let's look at Adam and his friends, and the ways in which nature, nurture, culture and chance have shaped their behaviour and their learning. We also need to look at the sort of provision Adam needs in his early years at nursery and at school. This will contribute to the 'nurture and culture' that will help him to make the best of his cleverness and may help to counteract the negative aspects of the life chances he has experienced as well as the genetic make-up that has thus far directed the growth of his brain.

As with all the boys in this book, all four influences will have an effect on Adam, but nature is the first driving force that will affect his disposition throughout his life. Genetic material in his cells will determine his height, eye colour and other features of his appearance, giving him family likenesses to his parents and siblings. His genes will also determine not just his sex, but the gender balance, and how much his behaviour is driven by testosterone. The effect of foetal testosterone on his developing brain will only trigger the tendencies already there.

Adam is a typical 'deconstructor', as are many children, and particularly many boys. The need to know how things work, what they are made from, whether they come apart, what they will do, which are all drivers to early learning, and boys seem more likely to become obsessed with both construction and deconstruction.

Research tells us that from their very first months of life, boys behave very differently from girls as they interact with their environment and the objects they are offered by their family and society. When little boys are given dolls, they are much more likely to use the doll as a tool, to bash, hit and react with the environment around them. They will try to remove the dolls' limbs and head, poke at their eyes, and generally explore them as objects. Boys' brains drive them towards moving objects. Visual stimuli will affect their brain growth, and their endless drive to find out how things work, is embedded in the structure of their brains. Boys naturally behave as mini-scientists, exploring and testing everything in their environment.

Girls, with their more highly developed sense of empathy and higher levels of oestrogen and oxytocin (the caring chemical) in their brains and bodies are likely to hold the doll, 'talk' to it, look closely at its face and eyes, hug and touch it in a gentle way. Girls naturally behave as mini-nurturers and carers, even when they are very young, and some boys who have a more feminine position on the gender spectrum may do so too. The level of testosterone in a boy's body will have a direct effect on his interest in construction and deconstruction, in caring or experiment, in objects or people.

This drive to explore, experiment and deconstruct is important not only to boys but to the human race, and it has been named 'boy energy' by Michael Gurian who describes it is an important influence on the development of the human race: 'If we can agree to call this kind of energy "boy energy" we can probably also agree that it is one of the greatest assets of a civilisation. Our homes are built by it. Our roads are laid down in its vision. Our rocket ships fly because of it.' Michael Gurian, *The Minds of Boys* (Jossey Bass 2005)

The need to mix and make 'potions' is also a feature of some boys' behaviour. Construction, deconstruction and changing things by mixing, are features of the early years of education, where the boys often take over the bricks, the construction toys and the 'making' and 're-making' of found materials indoors and outside. It is likely to be a group of boys that gets involved in ropes, tyres, guttering, crates and planks, arranging and rearranging these to make waterways, camps, dens and structures.

On a smaller scale, Lego becomes a fixation with some boys, and the fact that Lego and other construction toys can be made and re-made is part of its attraction. For other boys, liquid soap and loo roll in the bathroom, water in the sand, sand in the water, mixing paint colours, dipping their biscuit in milk until it falls apart and making mud pies are all fascinating occupations. These pursuits may be extremely frustrating for the practitioners, when materials and resources are used in such combinations, but are essential to growing scientists.

'Kailin and Shawn worked together in the block area to build a precarious structure that was approximately four feet tall and encompassed a floor area of about 50 square feet. During that time they were constantly confronted with challenges of balance, decision of purpose and use of the blocks... The result was a complex building that incorporated over a hundred blocks, cars and play figures.' Kathi, a teacher quoted in *Boys and Girls Learn Differently*, Michael Gurian, (Jossey Bass 2002)

Most practitioners are women – grown-up girls who like order and purpose. For most girls, water in the home corner teapot is for making cups of tea, dolls are for mothering, soap is for washing and mud is for walking round! Is this nature, nurture or culture? Does the pink tee shirt with 'Little Princess' for a girl, or the red one with 'Here's Trouble' for a boy make a difference to children's behaviour, or does it just reinforce a natural leaning towards one type of behaviour over another?

Recent brain research seems to indicate that culture (the messages we get in life and from the media) will reinforce a natural disposition, not create it; and the additional influence of chance (where nurture or culture takes place, who is the dominant parent, whether or not the child is born into a family where experiment is valued and encouraged) makes for a complexity that is almost impossible to unscramble.

Like Paul, Adam's position on the gender spectrum is towards the male extreme, he is a boyish boy, and a PET or MRI scan would probably help us to see the following features, and tensions between his strengths (his 'clevernesses') and the demands that early education are placing on him:

- The production of dopamine makes Adam a risk taker and experimenter. Like Paul, he takes action with little thought for the outcomes. However, unlike Paul, Adam's impulsiveness is smaller scale. He is fascinated by what things do when he takes them apart, or mixes them up. He will get involved in construction and deconstruction of anything, including pop-up books, bikes and magic potions, and the immediacy of his actions sometimes gets him into trouble.

- Spatial-mechanical stimulation, moving in space while thinking and learning, is something that most boys need and respond to, and Adam is on the extreme of this group too. He works best when he is actively involved in something that interests him, and 'hands-on' physical activity means more to him than sedentary, social activity. A higher level of blood flow in his brain drives him to activity, and even when he is listening or reading, he will be moving, fiddling, fidgeting, usually unconsciously. Try to make him keep still and his thinking will freeze too.

- Adam's fascination with objects and what they can do is a 'boy cleverness'. He is much more likely than most girls to focus on objects rather than people, and this will be apparent in his choice of toys and books, preferring mechanical toys and non-fiction books.

- Like most boys, Adam's corpus callosum, the 'superhighway' linking his left and right brain is less developed and less active than in most girls. This means he is less able to multitask, but much better at focussing on one thing. Adam spends much of his time making links in his right brain, often referred to as the 'Big Picture hemisphere' where action, space, images and objects influence behaviour. He will take much longer than many girls and some other boys to move into and fully develop the left side of his brain, the side where words, meaning, logic and order are used to enhance learning and thinking. This 'cleverness' of single focus remains a feature of boys' brains into manhood, enabling them to concentrate on their interests and their jobs.

The Cleverness of Boys

'Adult males climb higher in life because they are generally more ruthless.' Peter A Lawrence, *Men, Women, and Ghosts in Science* (Public Library of Science)

Adam will often choose to play alone, and his level of concentration on self-initiated activities is often very high. His single mindedness can make him inflexible in cooperative play, as he has a very clear idea of what he wants to do, and sometimes resists offers of help from others. He will spend long periods of time on one activity, and will be reluctant to respond to externally imposed timetables such as 'clearing up time'. If we ask his parents, they may say that Adam has always been an active child, and always interested in building and demolishing. He has a huge box of Lego at home, and plays for hours, making complex models of spaceships, vehicles and machines. His mother will also say that Adam can often be found quietly making 'mixtures' in the kitchen – something that gets him into trouble when he decides to raid the fridge and cupboards for ingredients!

- Adam probably has more cells in his brain that are associated with visual learning, and they aid the movement of messages from the eyes to the brain. This is probably why Adam differs in his behaviour from his more outgoing younger brother, being a watcher, not a do-er or showman, although he is just as energetic in the garden. He is quietly focused and will become distracted from family life as he becomes involved in his own activities, often getting diverted from meals or dressing for school by the visual stimulus he gets from the objects in his room or the classroom. He is not passive, just determined.

- A position near, but not at the far end of the extreme of the 'hunter' continuum of boys, will make Adam restless, but in a less obvious way. Where Paul is centre stage, Adam is active in the background. His scientific experiments are undertaken quietly, on a smaller scale. He is not being deliberately disobedient, even though it must seem so to the outsider – he is just focused, and when his agenda demands his attention he seems totally unable to respond. Adam's testosterone levels are high, but they are channelled into quiet, concentrated activity, and even his fidgeting may be under cover. Despite his solitary periods, and few close friends, Adam is a good 'pack member', who contributes to group activities with other boys, and is often a quiet leader in the more complex and investigative projects they undertake. He is also more than willing to get involved in the rough and tumble of games and minor physical power struggles.

- Adam's obsession with experiment is a real strength in his learning. Of course, he has preferred activities, but in these he takes not just pleasure, not just enthusiasm but joy in learning from the activities he chooses himself. He will follow up his own activities in discussions with other children, his parents and practitioners, and the things he learns, he really remembers. Despite what might be called his 'selective hearing' he remembers a great deal of the information he hears and discovers. His questions can be repetitive and sometimes seem irrelevant, but he is obsessed with checking out and confirming what he is learning. Of course, the adults who live and work with him often wish their priorities were as important to Adam as his own!

Boys like Adam have been described as those 'Boys who gain their toughness and tenderness by pushing through the seams and edges others may not see, or may fear' Michael Gurian *The Minds of Boys* (Jossey Bass 2005). He has a brain like Will Parry in Philip Pullman's *The Subtle Knife* (Scholastic), who experiments with alternative views and ways of organising and understanding the physical world. He makes things only to take them apart, builds things only to knock them down again, then builds them again, but better! Lego is made for these boys, and many, given the right nurture and culture, and good chances in life may become the next generation of scientists, perfumiers or chefs, making the ordinary extraordinary by mixing things in new ways.

Other influences

If he could follow his own path through days and weeks, Adam would construct, combine, reorganise and re-order his environment over and over again, but the adults in his life have other plans. They clear up, organise and tidy his laboratory and his day, and he sometimes responds with a tantrum of frustration.

Before he started school, Adam had much more flexibility to create and dismantle in peace. His good fortune included the chance of being born in a family where creativity and concentration have high value; he was able to pursue projects for as long as he wished, and leave them from day to day. His mother works part-time, and is not obsessed with housework. She is also distracted by Adam's younger brother, who is a much more demanding child. On her days at home with Adam when he was under four, she often left unfinished projects such as her huge collection of family photos or a pile of cookery books on the dining table, pushing these aside to make room for their lunch, or to bake cakes together. His dad is always in the garage, making and mending things, fixing bikes and lawn mowers, and leaving these in bits for days and weeks.

Such a creative household was an ideal setting for Adam, but it did not prepare him for the constraints of school! Nursery and reception experience proved acceptable to him, with new opportunities and plenty of time for self-initiated learning and discovery, with mud and sand to mix, new construction toys to explore and other boys to play with. He was also very interested in the non-fiction books in the library and the new possibilities offered in malleable and outdoor materials, although what he described as 'That music!' at packing away time sometimes made life very difficult. Adam's solution to this was often to go 'under cover' at this time, disappearing into a quiet corner and continuing his own agenda while the others got on with the demands of the day.

The good days are those when his agenda and that of the adults coincide, or at least can be managed together, as in the day he discovered dinosaur eggs. Adam's enthusiasm and ideas, carried over into the following day and a satisfactory conclusion, proved to be a triumph of his joy in learning, and this helped his teacher to forgive the other incidents when his experiments were less acceptable.

However, Adam will soon move into the primary classes, and managing his 'clevernesses' will need just as much careful thought as dealing with Paul. If we trample on his enthusiasm and insist on adherence to the programme, we risk driving him into submission, removing that spark of joy in learning and damaging his motivation. With encouragement, Adam's clevernesses may blossom into something creative and unique.

How to recognise and value the strengths of boys like Adam

Adam is clever at single focus, hands-on learning and experiment. His powers of concentration and creativity are exceptional. He needs an educational programme that capitalises on these, helping him to maintain his concentration and interest, and using these skills and ideas as starting points for learning the skills he will need in future. A combined curriculum, where projects and topics help children to make connections and use their emerging skills will suit Adam well, and this sort of curriculum is now extending from the early years into primary classes. Joined-up thinking and learning suit

Adam's style, so it is a fortunate chance that the school he attends is moving swiftly in this new direction.

It is now well recognised that despite their boisterous behaviour, and apparent disregard for adults, boys need firm and clear boundaries and to know 'who is in charge'. This is true at home and at school, so adults should make sure Adam knows what is expected of him! However, the adults who work with him currently know that the next few years could prove a different thing entirely. Sympathetic and skilled primary teachers could make efforts to respond to his needs for time and space to experiment, but the frustrations of an imposed timetable, group activities and particularly the increasing amount of time spent sitting still and listening will be a testing time for him.

Adam's parents are pleased that he is still enthusiastic about school, and has time for all his interests. However, they are concerned for the future, and want to do everything they can to maintain the balance between his individual interests and the skills and knowledge of the school curriculum. They work with the teachers to develop some of the strategies that will help Adam and the school to maintain his enthusiasm as he moves into primary classes:

- Adam needs to adjust to the demands of the school timetable. He finds this very frustrating, and hates having to stop his projects at pack-away time. This adjustment will take time, but meanwhile, the following might help:
  - Give an early warning of packing-up time. Staff need to make sure they tell Adam when he has five or ten minutes left, by finding where he is and getting his attention as they give the warning. Adam gets so involved in his projects that he needs individual contact to avoid frustration and even tantrums.
  - When possible, provide a space for 'Work in Progress' and give him the option of keeping his Lego model, brick construction or experiment until later or overnight. This demonstrates adult value for his projects, and gives him a sense of commitment and continuity.
  - Keep group times short and focused, and include plenty of movement and hands-on materials. This will help Adam, and most other boys to maintain interest. Use the materials he enjoys to enhance adult-led activities in your group times. Bricks, blocks, tubes and other construction materials can contribute to language and mathematical tasks. Take group times into the construction area, where Adam will feel at home.
  - Use a camera to record some of the construction (and deconstruction) projects and use these for discussions and displays. Reward his creativity by asking him to explain his projects to others in the group.

The Cleverness of Boys

- Adam is fascinated by mixing and changing things, so he needs plenty of challenges with resources that are acceptable and interesting, varied and constructive:
  - Provide plenty of problem solving activities, surprises and opportunities for creativity by 'planting' objects in unusual places or asking questions that lead to investigations. Offer small items for fixing, constructing, dismantling; and plenty of glue, tape, fasteners and other resources for making and creating.
  - Cooking is a great activity for children like Adam. Simple mixing, making and changing of food ingredients is the best introduction to science.
  - There are also endless simple practical activities that involve mixing and separating: mixing paint; making paste; adding water to sand or corn-flour; separating mixtures of pasta shapes or different types of seeds; sorting screws and washers; pouring sand, water or gloop; digging in mud.
  - Making waterways, marble runs or other small scale constructions and working models from recycled materials is another way of encouraging Adam and his friends to explore their interests in experiment and construction. As they get older, add some challenges to these simple activities so they really have to think.
  - When you go on walks or visits, offer some collecting bags. 'Found' and natural materials are good additions to more traditional construction sets as are recycled or 'junk' materials, and will test their skills of fixing, joining, balancing and creating.

- Like Paul, Adam is very good at focusing on one thing, but he is more likely to do this quietly and often un-noticed in a busy school or setting:
  - Give him plenty of time for activities he is interested in, but be clear about the times when he can follow his own interests and when you expect him to help others with clearing up, or come to group times when you need him. Praise him when he gets this right, and remember that boys need more reminders, in fewer words than many girls do.
  - Praise and acknowledgement is vital to the wellbeing of all children, but particularly for boys. Make sure everyone knows what the rules are, and when the ownership of learning is in their own hands. If Adam disappears at clearing-up time to follow his own interests, he needs to be reminded of the rules, even though his activities might fascinate or amuse you! Praise him for contributing to 'community tasks' such as packing away.

Given the support of his parents and the practitioners in the early years, Adam made a successful transfer to primary school. He is still inclined to go to what his Year 2 teacher calls 'Planet Adam' as he becomes engrossed in the details of how a spider's legs work, rather than following the task he has been given.

His teacher recognises and builds on his scientific and technological strengths, she encourages his detailed labelled diagrams of the things he is learning, instead of expecting lengthy writing. She fosters his interest in non-fiction books, particularly those about animals and the natural world, and scientific subjects. She has worked with the local librarian to find science books with text at his reading level, and these travel from home to school and back almost every day.

At home, Adam has become a proficient cook, making not only his own, but his brother's packed lunch every day. In the evenings and at weekends he works with his mum on her latest project – an allotment, where he is building a complex watering system, or with his dad who is still dismantling things in the garage!

Donovan the sportsman

Donovan's story

There was nothing that Donovan hated more than rain! Rain meant that the grass was out of commission, and as the headteacher would only allow football on the grass, Donovan's existence was reduced to one of agonising frustration. As far as he was concerned, life without football was simply not worth living. He played football at every possible opportunity with whoever was prepared to play, and usually there was no shortage of takers as Donovan was much admired by the other boys for his immense skill at the game.

In fact, Donovan was popular all round, with many of the girls claiming him as their 'boyfriend!' But football was his life! When he wasn't playing it he was watching it or reading about it. It was perhaps fortuitous that the school colours were the same as the football strip of his beloved team, because had they not been he would probably have refused to wear them! If it wasn't claret and blue, then it wasn't worth wearing!

It didn't help either that he lived on the eighth floor of a high rise block of flats, which for someone as energetic as Donovan was something of an endurance test, not to mention the consequences to his long-suffering mother who had to deal with all that contained energy on a daily basis. Donovan was never happier than when playing football. When he walked to school in the morning his favourite football would be clamped to his chest (he had several, all of which would be his 'best' ball for particular reasons at particular times).

Like a little puppy, Donovan was never still, although when it came to skilled coordination of limbs, any comparison with a puppy was inappropriate. Donovan's control over his limbs was astonishing for one so young. He could do things with a ball that the rest of us could only dream about. He could also move at the speed of light – one minute you saw him – the next you didn't! But never have I seen him move so fast as the morning when he received the best news he had ever had, and he couldn't wait to tell me.

'Mrs Bayley,' he screamed as he hurtled across the outdoor area. 'Guess what...' He skidded to a breathless halt at the door. 'Me dad's going to take me to the cup final... he's got tickets and he's going to take me... he phoned up last night to say!'

'Well that's fantastic Donovan!' I said. I was so pleased for him and remembered how excited he had been when his team got to the final. However, secretly I just hoped that his dad kept his promise. He'd promised things before and not carried them out, but never in the context of something as important as this. If he let Donovan down this time I just knew that the little boy would be devastated and, even at this early stage, began to pray that it was a promise that would be kept!

Throughout that day and the days that followed Donovan talked of nothing else, and when he was forced to do something other than playing football he was writing about it or painting pictures of it! When he got a bit muddled up about how many 'sleeps' were left before the cup final day finally arrived, we made a chart so that when he got to school each morning he could tick them off. There was nobody who didn't know about his impending visit to the cup final. He had even planned what he was going to wear and made a list of what he needed to take with him. Never before had I seen him so deliriously happy.

When his mum brought him each morning we reflected on what an amazing effect the forthcoming visit had had on him. For Donovan, while he was no real trouble in school, could be very challenging with his mum! 'Donovan's been a little angel Mrs Bayley,' she said one morning. 'He's done absolutely everything I've asked him to. It's made such a difference, his dad taking a bit of interest in him for once! I only hope nothing goes wrong.'

'I'm sure it won't,' I said reassuringly. I just hoped I was right!

There was no doubt about it, Donovan had seemed a lot more settled recently and perhaps this time his dad really was sincere about his intentions and would come up with the goods. I watched Donovan as he played football outside. He was just a little version of his dad: tall, lean and athletic, with a crop of curly black hair, and it has to be said that Donovan doted on his dad, in spite of the fact that he had let him down on numerous occasions. It was rare for his dad to ever pick him up from school so I was more than a little surprised when, in the middle of story time, Donovan ran to the window shrieking. 'Look everyone, look! That's my dad's car!' In spite of my protestations everyone surged to the window to look, and sure enough, there was Donovan's dad's somewhat ostentatious sports car parked right over the yellow zig-zags just outside the school gates!

'Wow!' shrieked Jamie Gilbert.

'Cool, or what?' echoed Amit Patel.

'That's magic!' declared David Jones, as the rest of the children looked on in amazement.

'Yeah and guess what,' announced Donovan excitedly. 'We're going to the cup final in that car!'

The rest of the children were clearly impressed. I did my best to usher them back to the carpet in order to resume my reading of *The Gruffalo*, which although it was one of the children's favourite stories, could not compete with Donovan's dad's car!

Once back on the carpet, things settled down a bit, at least they did until it was time for the parents and carers to collect the children. As Donovan's dad swaggered through the door, Donovan catapulted himself across the room nearly knocking down everyone in his path. 'Steady Donovan,' I said anxiously as he and his friends gathered round this tall man, with questions about his car, the cup final and the label on his trainers. I looked on as Donovan swelled with pride. I exchanged pleasantries with his dad, taking him to the other side of the room to clear the pathway to the door.

'Donovan is *so* excited about going to the cup final! In some ways I shall be glad when it's over and we can get him back down to earth again!' I said jokingly. Donovan's dad, who was a man of few words as far as teachers were concerned smiled, as he accompanied the ecstatic Donovan out of the room. 'Bye Mrs Bayley,' shouted Donovan. 'Only three days to go now!'

As I tidied up that afternoon I thought about how unfair I had been to imagine that Donovan's dad would let him down. I was sure that this time, all would be well, so it was with some misgivings that I noticed the next morning that Donovan had not turned up for school. This was almost unheard of. In fact, his attendance record was generally exemplary! However, all was to be revealed later that day. Just after the other children had gone home, Donovan's mum came into the classroom dragging a very downcast Donovan behind her. She was looking incredibly worried as well as very pale and tired.

'What is it?' I asked. 'Is something wrong?'

Donovan's mum nodded her head. 'I'm afraid it is', she said, and went on to explain. 'Donovan's dad came for tea last night, then, when he was going down the stairs to go home he slipped and fell and he's broken his thigh. We've been at the hospital all night and most of the day, and I'm afraid he's going to be in there for some time!'

'Oh, I'm so sorry to hear that,' I said, not at all registering the implications for his son.

'And now we can't go to the cup final!' said Donovan, bursting into floods of tears.

'Oh Donovan!' implored his mum. 'Don't start that again. There's nothing we can do about it and that's that! Come on, we'd better get home.'

'Well take care, and if there's anything we can do to help do let us know,' I added.

As they disappeared through the door I couldn't help feeling sorry for them. It was going to mean a lot of trips on the bus to and from the hospital. For although they were no longer together, Donovan's mum and dad were on reasonably friendly terms and I was sure she would be taking Donovan to visit his dad, and as for Donovan I was afraid that he might be inconsolable.

The following day my fears were to be realised. Although Donovan was in school, he may as well not have been for all he got out of it. He didn't even want to play football and for most of the day remained slumped in the book corner every bit the picture of misery. Still, these things happen, and as he was quite resilient I was sure he would get over it. Anyway there was nothing that could be done about it, or at least that's what I thought. The hand of fate had a different plan!

That night I was due to go to a birthday party at a friend's house, and I had to admit that as I was feeling somewhat tired I didn't really want to go. However, she was a good friend so I wasn't going to let her down, and never before have I been so glad that I made the effort.

Unbeknown to me, my friend's daughter, who was also at the party had a new and somewhat well-known boyfriend. At least, when I say well-known, he was well-known to anybody who followed the fortunes of the football team in claret and blue! He was called Craig and he played centre forward! Anyway, when I was introduced to him I found myself telling him about what had happened to Donovan, and so touched was he by the plight of the disappointed five-year-old that he promised to visit school the next day and see what he could do to help! I couldn't have been more grateful and thanked him profusely. I don't know about Donovan, this had made *my* day, so much so that I really enjoyed the rest of the party.

The next day, I didn't say anything to Donovan, who still looked incredibly miserable, just in case anything happened and Craig was unable to make it to school. The day progressed, Donovan sat in the book corner, and it must have been about two o'clock that the secretary arrived to tell us that we had a visitor who was looking for a game of football! I relayed this to Donovan who looked up half-heartedly and said he would play if they wanted to. Apathetically, he fetched his football from the top of the cupboard, but when he turned round and saw Craig standing in the doorway his eyes came out like organ stops! Donovan recognised him instantly.

'You don't need that mate,' said Craig. 'I've bought this one for you.' With that he presented Donovan with a ball that had been signed by every one of his beloved team.

The rest is history. Donovan had one of the best afternoons of his life. The kindly Craig stayed for the rest of the afternoon playing football with Donovan and his friends and when Donovan's mum came to collect him at the end of the day he could hardly wait to tell her what had happened.

'Oh mum,' he said, bouncing up and down with excitement. 'It was fantastic!' Just wait till I tell Dad. He's never going to believe this is he?' Compared to the afternoon's experience, a visit to the match, even if he'd been going to go with his dad, and even if it was a cup final, had paled into insignificance. The next day, Donovan was quite back to his old self, except he looked almost as if he had grown an inch or two overnight!

How Donovan's brain affects his behaviour

Donovan will be well known to readers – he is the boy with a single mind! And that mind is on sport. The group of boys he usually plays with are active, energetic and full of life, as long as they are also on the move. Sitting still is really hard for them, testosterone makes them fidgety and as they probably have more muscle bulk and more red blood cells than some other boys and certainly most girls, they move constantly. Whatever they are doing, they move – as they speak, as they read, as they sing, and probably even when they sleep. The active life they lead and their boundless energy give them stamina, agility, and a sense of team or 'pack' which invisibly as well as physically binds the group together.

Unlike Adam, who often operates alone, Donovan's position as 'leader of the pack' is very important to him. Staying within the pack and impressing them with physical prowess, experiences, even the brand name on your trainers or the team you support, is vital to continuing membership.

Work on gender characteristics now suggests that Donovan's brain and body are not much different from his prehistoric ancestors, and some of his behaviour will give credibility to these theories. Boys like Donovan find it difficult to maintain eye contact, their brains and vision encourage long sight for hunting, not close attention to faces and expressions. They find it easier to talk when next to you, rather than face to face, and will often talk as they walk or run in the pack. Because they have stamina and strength for the chase, and this encourages the development of gross motor skills, their fine motor movement is sometimes clumsy (as in the story about Adam) or uncontrolled. Colour is important to Donovan, and it's interesting that researchers also find that across continents the majority of boys really do prefer blue and the majority of girls really do prefer pink! The theory is that hunters would be attracted by blue because water attracts animals to hunt, and gatherers (the females) would be attracted by the pinks and reds of fruits and berries in their environment.

Donovan needs plenty of action and movement, and finds the quieter more sedentary activities in the setting frustrating and lacking in fulfilment. Outdoor activity is vital to his wellbeing and the 'social glue' he gets from his friends is reinforced when they play competitive/collaborative games such as football. However, it would be good to remind ourselves that boys like Donovan also need to drop into what some researchers have described as 'rest state', particularly after intense physical or mental activity, a state which can be observed in many boys who 'drift', 'gaze', or drop out of concentration.

Donovan is a tough boy in some ways, but in others, he is very fragile. His father means a lot to him, and the separation of his parents has left him vulnerable. Steve Biddulph in *Raising Boys* (Thorsons 1997) explores the needs of young boys for a father figure, and describes the consequences of a missing father figure as DDD (Dad Deficit Disorder):

'At around six, little boys seem to "lock onto" their dad or stepdad, or whichever male is around and want to be with him, learn from him, and copy him. They want to 'study how to be a male'. If a dad ignores his son at this time, the boy will often launch an all-out campaign to get his attention.

Boys may steal, wet the bed, act aggressively at school and develop any number of problem behaviours, just to get dad to take an interest.'

Donovan not only idolises his dad, but will forgive him almost anything, overlooking his shortcomings and broken promises, greeting him with adoration when he chooses to appear, and always proud to show him off to his friends.

Key elements of the brain

Looking more closely at some of these features of Donovan's brain and behaviour, we can begin to understand what makes him the way he is. He is a unique combination of nature (with genetic features of his mother and his father, both African Caribbean); nurture (the care given by a lone mother, a close extended family and during inconsistent contact with his dad); culture (where celebrity status of football and the need for the 'right' clothes and kit is a huge pressure) and chance (the chance effect of a parental break-up, getting the right teacher, or a meeting at a party).

Donovan's mum could easily destroy his relationship with his dad, but she doesn't. Even though she hasn't read the research, she instinctively knows how important fathers are to young boys. Donovan's need for safety, security and love are met in a loving relationship with his mother who never undermines his relationship with his dad, and combined with Donovan's forgiving nature, his dad is always sure of a welcome.

Allan Schore from UCLA was among the first to notice what happens when a child doesn't get enough touch, from the mother but also from others including fathers:

While the mother-child dyad maintains primacy because of its psychobiological underpinnings in survival and optimal development, the child cultivates an array of "affectional bonds" that include, most importantly, the father or partner, as well as other members of the network of close family and friends. Attunement in each of these relationships is intensely important because the child is always taking in new information and being shaped by the world. Just as the mother's role is to assist in the child's development, so is the role of every other primary person in the child's life. While attachment theory centres on a primary figure, typically the mother, as the bedrock of the child's health and wellbeing, this does not occur in a vacuum, nor to the exclusion of fathers and partners. Often, in the progression of infant development, the initial role of fathers focuses on support of the mother in her attempt to care for their baby. But it does not stop there. As the baby gains in abilities, the father becomes more central, and his role often evolves into the safe launching point for the child's accelerated forays into the external world.' Allan N Schore, 'Effects of a Secure Attachment Relationship on Right Brain Development, Affect Regulation and Infant Mental Health,' *Infant Mental Health Journal* 22, 1–2 (2001).

Donovan's close family, which includes both pairs of grandparents and many cousins, uncles and aunts, support him in feeling confident and cared for, enabling him to be generous in his feelings when his father lets him down.

Donovan is probably towards the masculine end of the gender spectrum. He has plenty of testosterone to fuel his sporting activities, a powerful and muscular body, inherited from his father's family, and a real need to be part of a 'pack'. Investigation of the structure of his brain would probably uncover these features:

- A position at the masculine end of the gender spectrum will result in the sort of single-mindedness and persistence Donovan shows in maintaining his interest in sport and particularly football. Dopamine in the brain often results in extreme territoriality and social hierarchies. However, Donovan has developed a way of channelling the dopamine into structured activities with clear rules of engagement. This technique is usually much slower to develop in boys than girls, who quickly begin to establish hierarchies and rules in their games, so it is an early advantage for him.

- Being a boy will mean that the links between Donovan's left and right brain hemispheres are slower to develop. He will still be concentrating thinking and linking brain cells in the right hemisphere, where action, pattern and movement dominate. However, he has also spent a lot of time with his mother since his father left, and this has resulted in early development of empathy and using the language of feelings. This contact helps him to deal with frustration and disappointment more easily than many other boys of his age, without resorting to tantrums or violence.

- Male features of the brain will also affect Donovan's relationship with other boys, making the pack and loyalty to its members absolutely central. Such is the feeling between groups of boys like Donovan that they often operate without much language, using single words, noises and physical demonstrations of affection. This may make them seem more like puppies or cubs than boys!

- The structure of Donovan's brain and body, as well as his genes result in good gross motor coordination. He can run, jump, kick a ball and throw better than many other boys of his age, and his movement around spaces both indoors and outside is controlled and poised, sometimes reminding people of a dancer, rather than a sportsman.

- Donovan is enthusiastic and excitable but the nurture in his family, the models provided by his parents, and his relatively early ability to control impulses means he rarely lets his enthusiasms get out of hand – with the exception of cup final tickets of course!

Other influences

Donovan is a popular and likeable member of his group, well known across the school, even among older children who admire his sporting skills (and his dad's car!). The range of his skills and personal attributes enable him to balance the demands of his teacher with his enthusiasm for sport and his friends. He has yet to adjust to being popular with girls, and finds it difficult to manage their admiration and desire to be his friends too. The model of his father may well be influencing how he feels about the opposite sex. School has taken him from his rather intense, high-rise life with mum, which could have become claustrophobic and limiting, and has given him friends, space and purpose.

At home, Donovan's 'clevernesses' are appreciated by his extended family. Cousins and uncles visit at the weekend to play football in the spaces at the foot of the block of flats. After his mum fetches him from After School Club, he spends hours kicking his favourite football against the wall of the balcony, until it's time to sit and snuggle with his mum under a blanket on the settee, watching DVDs, reading the newspaper or telling stories together.

Nursery and then a flexible and play-based reception class enlarged Donovan's horizons and he flourished there. His reading and writing skills are improving, particularly now he has found the sports section in the library, and he has developed a real interest in numbers and shapes. However he is still more interested in action than sedentary activities and has very definite preferences in the activities he enjoys and those he doesn't.

At first reading, Donovan may not seem to present many problems for his family or his school, but he is still vulnerable to the pressures of the education system and particularly to 21st century culture. He is a black boy from a lone-parent family, living in an urban environment and qualifying for free school meals. Here are some statistics and social trends for Great Britain that may affect Donovan as he grows up:

- The proportion of children living in lone-parent families in Great Britain more than tripled between 1972 and spring 2006 to 24%. Lone mothers head around nine out of ten lone-parent families. 48% of Black Caribbean households with dependent children were headed by a lone parent.

- 39% of all families accepted as homeless were lone mothers with children. In England in 2004/05 (the latest year for which these data are available), there were 13 times as many lone mothers with dependent children accepted as there were lone fathers.

- There are also variations in achievement by free school meal eligibility. Data from England shows that pupils who were not eligible for free school meals generally performed better than those who were eligible at each Key Stage.

- In urban areas, black boys are more likely to be stopped and searched by police, more likely to be arrested and this is likely to be for firearms or drugs. Overall, black people accounted for 14% of those stopped and searched in 2004/05. (Office for National Statistics, *Social Trends*, No. 37, 2007)

Of course, these life chances are not certainties for Donovan, but living in an urban area and with a strong inclination to belong to a 'pack' or 'team' puts him at risk compared to some of his more fortunate friends.

His mother did well at school, loved English and read widely, but never took up the opportunity to go to college because no one in her family had ever had higher education. Her relationship with Donovan's father, and pregnancy at a young age, finally put paid to her aspirations for her own education. She has pinned her hopes on Donovan and his future.

One of the indicators of the achievements of children is their mother's aspirations: 'There is evidence to suggest that some Black African children are among those more likely to experience a poor quality home-learning environment, as defined by the Effective Provision of Pre-school Education (EPPE) research. What takes place in the home – particularly in relation to parents supporting the learning of their children – can be more influential in producing good educational outcomes than socio-economic status.' (EPPE research cited in *Fairness and Freedom: The final report of the Equalities Review 2007*)

Donovan is lucky that his mother has high hopes for him and is prepared to put time into making sure he achieves them, but it will be a difficult job and events and attitudes may work to reduce his current high levels of motivation and enthusiasm.

On the other hand, Donovan's father is honest in saying he was 'a bit of a lad' at school, didn't do very well and got into 'bad company' when he left. He has had a series of jobs, but is not prepared to divulge what they are! However, he is determined to support Donovan and make sure he has a good education, although he secretly wishes that a talent scout from a national football club will spot him on the football field!

How to recognise and value the strengths of boys like Donovan

The teachers and the head of Donovan's school are very aware of what might happen to pupils in the future, and are keen to make sure that every child in the school has the skills and knowledge they need to succeed. Donovan's mother and father are aware of the risks that face him as he grows up, and are very willing to do what they can to help. They attend parent discussions together to discuss Donovan's progress and his future. They try to maintain the consistency in their expectations of Donovan's behaviour, and want him to do well.

Donovan's 'clevernesses' include his strong commitment to his friends, his popularity, enthusiasm and energy, his loyalty and forgiveness, particularly for his father, and his ability to concentrate on one thing at a time, developing real passion for his current interests. The issues for those who live and work with him are to encourage him to expand his horizons by working with children outside his immediate circle; to embrace other activities and occupations; and to build his strength of character so he can succeed against the cultural and social pressures he will face as he grows up in an urban environment.

The strategies discussed with Donovan's parents and among the staff at school included these. Some of the issues are those that face all the children in the school, which has a catchment area of considerable difficulty and disadvantage. Others particularly suit Donovan and boys like him:

- A continuing interest in sport and team games is very important to Donovan and can be used as a trigger to learning.
  - Team playing and cooperation should permeate your work. Remember that teamwork is not only about sport. Give plenty of opportunities to work in groups and teams on other tasks and activities right across the curriculum. Make sure boys and girls get used to working in mixed groups, and support them as they learn to accept the differences between boys and girls and different members of the class.
  - Use all your contacts to bring visitors into your school or setting – local sportsmen and women; leaders of sports clubs or centres; football team captains from local clubs and schools; local youth leaders. Models of successful black boys and men will be very influential, but don't overdo this aspect, keep the representation broad!

- Donovan is beginning to be affected by social influences and pressures, such as designer clothing and cars. This pressure is bound to increase as he grows older, and the celebrity status of sport is very influential on behaviour, language and dress.
  - Take informal as well as more formal opportunities to talk to the whole class or group about designer labels and the pressures that children face in a consumer-led society. Talk about your own interests, discuss the language of advertising, the importance of being a thinking consumer, and help children to think objectively about the difference between what they *want* and what they *need* or can afford. The culture of celebrity is a very strong influence in children's lives, and recent surveys show worrying trends in young children's views so try to help them to think sensibly, even though the pressures are great:
    'Children under 10 think being a celebrity is the "very best thing in the

world" but do not think quite as much of God, a survey has revealed. The poll of just under 1,500 youngsters ranked "God" as their tenth favourite thing in the world, with celebrity, "good looks" and being rich at one, two and three respectively.' National Kids' Day Survey, Luton First (*Daily Mail*, December 2006)

- Donovan is developing a real interest in numbers and shapes, but is not really switched on to the sort of formal maths sessions recently implemented by the government. Despite the fact that they are not less able than other children, black boys are currently performing well below their peers from other ethnic groups across all areas of learning, including Problem Solving, Reasoning and Numeracy, at the end of the Early Years Foundation. 'There is no inherent reason why this group of children should do less well than their peers.' *Building Futures: Believing in children; A focus on provision for Black children in the Early Years* (DCSF 2009)
  - In *Building Futures, Believing in children; A focus on provision for Black children in the Early Years* (DCSF 2009) the following guidance is given: 'It is important to ensure that all Black children, especially Black boys, are able to make a positive start to their school careers. For many Black children this positive start occurs because of the strong foundation for learning set down in the home and then the combined, additional support from school and community. Some children, especially those from areas of social and economic disadvantage, will require support if they are to become and to remain safe from potential harm. Security and safety will allow them the space to explore and grow as learners and will do much to change the consequences for some of those young Black people for whom educational failure leads to social exclusion and worse.' For Donovan, this will be crucial to his success in school and after. Practitioners who are working with boys like Donovan will find the examples from practice in this guidance helpful in giving ideas for active involvement and diversity in practice.
  - Active maths, set in a problem solving environment will help Donovan and boys like him to maintain interest. Maths out of doors, or challenges linked to his interest in sport (using the sports pages of the newspaper or information about football teams) could also switch him on.
  - Offer lots of three-dimensional materials such as bricks, cubes, construction sets and recycled materials so he can explore shapes and structures in three dimensions. Moving as he learns, talks and reports back will all help Donovan to keep on task.

- Encourage him to plan before he starts on problem solving activities, using diagrams, mind maps and pictures to help his thinking. Boys can imagine shapes in space more easily than many girls, and need practice in recording them.

- Donovan's mum has taught him to talk about his feelings and emotions. She has encouraged him to be understanding, forgiving and loyal, particularly to his father and his extended family. This has enabled him to become a good team player with his friends at school. The adults at school need to continue to support his emotional development, recognising his early skills and attitudes and building on them:
  - Give all children opportunities to talk about their feelings. Some boys find this difficult, and will need more practice to feel secure in opening up and admitting how they feel. Stories, songs and rhymes can help, so can music and dancing, but remember to include songs and stories from a wide variety of backgrounds and cultures. Examples could include *So Much*, by Trish Cooke (Walker Books Ltd) *Amazing Grace* by Mary Hoffman (Frances Lincoln) and the Jamela stories by Niki Daly (Frances Lincoln) or using a 'Smileometer' to indicate how they are feeling.
  - Non-fiction books are popular with many boys and can be used effectively to develop literacy skills and a love of books and reading. Donovan is already an enthusiastic story-teller, and needs to have this skill recognised; he also needs opportunities to practise and expand his ability through role-play and story-telling sessions in his setting.

- The ability to focus on one thing at a time is both a 'cleverness' and a problem, depending on whether you are Donovan or an adult trying to work with him! Many boys have this ability to focus, and when most practitioners in the early years are female, this can cause problems. Like other boys in this book, Donovan needs time and understanding to avoid the frustration that builds up when expectations are too high:
  - Many boys like Donovan can concentrate for long periods on activities that capture their interest, and for Donovan this is football. Try to make child-initiated activity time as long as possible, and give energetic boys time to follow their current interests *before* you ask them to sit and listen. Plenty of space to run in groups and make noise will be vital, but this doesn't mean that boys take over the whole outdoor space. Learning to share and compromise is part of learning to live in a community.
  - Remember that large motor activity just before a spell of fine motor activity is a good strategy, so if you are going to embark on a

concentrated maths or phonics session, make sure Donovan and his friends have a physical activity just before you start – even a quick run round the playground or a group throwing and catching game will help to focus their attention.

- Donovan found it really difficult to cope with his disappointment when his dad went into hospital. On these occasions, it may be difficult to distract a child from their current mood, and they need time to withdraw and a space to be quiet as they learn to cope with their feelings. Of course, adults need to be on hand to talk and share thoughts, but sometimes being alone is a good thing.

All children, not just Black boys, need sensitive handling and understanding of their unique circumstances, families and life chances. Donovan is fortunate that he attends a school with a commitment to work closely with parents, recognising each child as an individual, with a unique mixture of strengths and needs. As Donovan moved through his primary years, he continued to be a team player, and maintained his bond with both his mother and his father. They are proud of his place in the school football team and his academic progress, particularly in maths, where he is the leading light of the school 'Mindstretchers Club'.

Leroy the leader

Leroy's story

Leroy sat on the carpet, his head in his hands, looking every bit the picture of misery. 'Come on,' I said encouragingly, 'there are lots of other things you can do in the outside area besides riding the bikes.'

'I know,' replied Leroy despondently, 'but all the other stuff we wanted to do is locked in the shed 'an all!'

'Well I'm very sorry about that,' I said with genuine sympathy, 'but it wasn't me that lost the key. You lot had it yesterday and you've obviously put it down somewhere and forgotten to put it back on the peg, and until it's found we won't be able to get anything out of the shed!'

'But Daniel said he gave it back to you Miss,' protested Leroy, obviously still in the grip of deep disappointment.

'I can assure you he didn't,' I said emphatically, 'because if he had done it would be back on the peg where it belongs! Now come on, there must be lots of other things you'd like to do.'

Leroy thought for a moment and then his face broke into a broad smile. 'Yeah, there is,' he said, suddenly recovering his good humour, 'I'm going to get everyone together and search for the key!' The next instant he had shot off the carpet like a bullet from a gun, and was soon outside organising everyone. 'Dan, you and Omar search the grass round the shed and me and Josh'll look in the flower beds. The rest of you do the play house and the concrete. And Nirwen, you go and ask Mrs Bayley if you and Tom can go round the classes and ask if anyone has found a key.'

I looked on, amazed at the way Leroy could mobilise the rest of the boys into immediate, frantic activity. I had to admit to feeling slightly envious, in the full knowledge that if I had asked them to do those things they'd have been far more reluctant! It didn't seem to matter whether he was organising a football game or a rota for the bikes, Leroy most definitely had clout! The other boys never seemed to question his judgement, even in situations where you might have expected at least one or two of the more thoughtful boys to have done so!

I thought back with interest to the events of the previous week, and as I did so, stifled a smile. We had been having some maintenance work done on the heating system in the unit, and Leroy and his associates had been much taken with the workmen who had arrived to carry out the work. They had watched in awe as the men pulled tools from the belts strapped around their waists and in no time at all had stripped radiators from the wall.

Moments later, Leroy and the gang were in the workshop area constructing belts from strips of material and card. Then they were off to the woodwork area where they availed themselves of hammers and screwdrivers to put in their belts, and finally, looking extremely pleased with themselves, they disappeared from the room. I remember thinking what a shame it was that we didn't have more male role models in the early years sector.

Some time later, as I addressed the task of supporting a three-year-old who was having difficulty getting two boxes to stick together, one of the nursery officers arrived in the room. She was brandishing a metal bracket in her hand and looking rather flustered. 'Have you seen what Leroy and co have done?' she asked, in outraged tones.

'No, I haven't,' I answered innocently.

'Well you'd better come and look,' she replied, 'and I hope you're good at putting radiators back on walls!' By the time I arrived in the soft play room, Leroy and friends were standing by the radiator looking somewhat confused, as if they didn't quite understand what all the fuss was about. Leroy looked at me. 'We were only trying to mend it so as it would work a bit more better,' he said defensively. Reminding myself that young children learn by listening, watching and copying, I patiently thanked Leroy and his friends for their efforts and explained that there were some jobs that just needed to be left to the professionals!

Bringing myself back to the present, I wondered how the search for the key was going. I noticed that the search party had come inside and was engaged in some kind of frantic activity in the writing area. 'Any luck with the key search?' I enquired, although I don't know why, because if the key had been found I'm sure that we would all have been instantly and noisily informed!

'Nope,' said Leroy, 'it ain't nowhere in the outside area. We've even searched all in the sand pit, so we're making some notices to put through people's doors to ask if anyone has found a key. I need to give 'em out at home time so everyone can deliver 'em on the way home! Maybe someone found the key last night when we'd all gone home and if they did they're most probably wondering what it's for, ain't they!'

'I tell you what,' I said, trying to be encouraging, 'when you've finished putting down what you want to say, why don't we give it to the school secretary to type out and photocopy?' The boys seemed to like that idea and at least that way I could ensure that the message would be understandable to the readers! So the message was duly typed and copied and at home time Leroy reminded me about the important task of distributing the letters. 'Now, you lot,' he urged everyone, 'make sure you deliver 'em to the neighbours on the way home and that'll be sure to get the key back and then tomorrow we'll be able to get the bikes and the balls and the ropes and all the other stuff out.' I so admired Leroy's optimism, but couldn't help feeling that he might just be disappointed by the time tomorrow morning came.

As suspected, once enquiries had been made the next morning, it became clear that the shed was going to remain locked for the foreseeable future! Nobody could throw any light on the whereabouts of the elusive key and the letters to the neighbours had not resulted in its sudden miraculous recovery. Leroy was clearly disturbed. 'Well what we going to do then Miss?' he asked seriously. 'How are we going to get into the shed to get all the stuff out?' I thought for a moment and then said, 'Look, we'll give it to the end of the week and then, if the key hasn't turned up we'll just have to get Tony (the site manager) to change the lock. And then, you'll all have to be a lot more careful with the key'.

'But we allus are careful Miss,' protested Leroy.

'Not careful enough!' I added with some irritation.

The rest of the week may have proved rather tiresome for Leroy and his associates, had it not been for a fabulously attractive distraction. In fact, such was the pull of this new pursuit that for the next two days the key was barely mentioned! We had a film crew in the unit! Sent in by the local authority that was making a film about early years practice in our area, they were heaven sent. Following the film crew around and pretending to be cameramen and sound technicians kept the boys busy for two whole days. They once again visited the workshop area where boxes and tubes were transformed into cameras and microphones, and even when the film crew had disappeared, the play continued for a further day.

I had hoped that the film crew play might see us through to the end of the week, but by Friday, Leroy was once again lamenting the disappearance of the key and the inability to access most of the equipment he loved the best. 'That naughty key must be somewhere,' he announced. 'We need to have another look. We need to dig down deeper in the sand pit and the garden. Come on men, let's go, and dig really, really deep this time!'

'Just mind the flowers,' I reminded them. We had grown lots of annuals in the garden and I could just see what might happen if the garden became the focus of too much overly enthusiastic digging.

'We will,' Leroy replied, not altogether reassuringly, 'but we just got to find that key!'

Throughout the rest of the day there was much frantic digging, during which all manner of missing objects were uncovered, although unfortunately, the key was not one of them. By the end of the day the boys were incredibly dirty and I have to say, somewhat gloomy. As they sat on the carpet at home time I applauded their efforts and assured them that I would speak to Tony about changing the locks before I went home.

'Will he do it before Monday?' asked Leroy.

'I'm sure he will if he can,' I said, suddenly feeling a rush of sympathy for Leroy, who lived in a small flat with no garden, and for whom the contents of the shed and the opportunities they afforded were extremely important.

'That's great then, 'cause we'll be able to get all the stuff out next week!'

When the children had gone I thought about all the things I needed to get done over the weekend. I sat down and made a list so that I could make sure that I took home everything I needed. Then I packed the car and set off, resolving to stop on the way home to collect some shopping and carry out one or two other errands. As I struggled out of the supermarket with several bags of shopping I remembered that I needed to go to the dry cleaners to pick up some stuff that had been there for most of the week. Imagine my surprise when I saw a brown envelope pinned to one of my jackets. 'What's in there?' I asked with interest.

'Oh,' explained the assistant, 'that's what we do when we find things that have been left in a pocket or have slipped into the lining.'

'Well now,' I said with surprise as I opened the envelope. 'Perhaps it's a 20 pound note!'

Before she could answer, something fell out of the envelope, making a clattering sound on the floor, and I looked down. There on the floor was the key to the shed! Apparently, there was a hole in the lining of my jacket and the key had dropped through. Daniel had actually been right, he *had* given me the key and it was *me* who had forgotten to replace it on its peg! Clearly, I had some apologising to do on Monday morning.

As I ate dinner that evening I reflected on how easy it can be for adults to fail to take children seriously. I hoped they wouldn't be too cross with me, although I wasn't really worried for I knew in my heart that Leroy and the gang were far too big-hearted to bear a grudge, and I was indeed right. When I made my confession on Monday morning Leroy simply fell about laughing, and we all laughed even more when Tony came in to tell us that he had changed the lock over the weekend. So, the reclaimed key was now totally useless! As Tony handed me two new keys to the shed, Leroy shouted, 'Don't give 'em to Mrs Bayley, she'll only lose 'em!'

'Well then Leroy,' I said, 'how can we make sure this doesn't happen again?'

The Cleverness of Boys

Leroy thought for a moment and then he said decisively, 'Put one on the peg, and give the other to Tony in case the peg one gets lost, and then if it does we'll 'ave a spare 'un!'

'That sounds very sensible to me,' I said, handing the keys to Leroy, who took one, and handed the other to Tony. 'Come on men,' he shouted, 'let's open the shed!' As Leroy ran off, followed by his gang I managed to stop myself saying, 'and don't forget to put the key back on the peg!' Why wouldn't he? It was too important for him not to!

How Leroy's brain affects his behaviour

Leroy is not a sportsman like Donovan, he is a different sort of leader – a leader of people – the sort of leader who gets people enthused and organised, keeps them focused and leads by example. He is already able to deploy members of his team, assign them jobs and trust them to report back to him. Given the right opportunities he could become the head of a research team, the leader of an expedition or an orchestra, a project manager or even a ringmaster! This sort of organisational ability is a result of having a particular mixture of genes and nurture that affect the structure and working of his brain.

Despite living with older twin sisters; a mum who is a carer in a residential home at weekends and in the evenings; a dad who works away from home during the week, running a sales team for a computer firm; and two very local grandmothers, Leroy is a very active and boyish boy. He seems little affected by his female dominated upbringing.

He gets much of his skill with language and in working with people from his dad, who won the Sales Team Leader of the Year award last year, but his genetic make-up and brain structure is complicated by the fact that his mother was born and brought up in Eastern Europe, and she still finds spoken English difficult, which sometimes frustrates her when she wants to talk to the elderly residents of the home or with Leroy's teachers. His grandmothers both speak Polish within the family and in their local community, and being bi-lingual will be an advantage for Leroy, keeping the language centres in his brain flexible and avoiding the neural pruning that single language speakers suffer.

The family still lives in a small flat with a very small garden, something that frustrates Leroy, who really does need to let off steam frequently. The park is nearby, but football and climbing are not the favourite interests of his sisters, or his grandmothers who take turns to provide after-school care. So Leroy's body is frustrated, encouraging his brain to produce more dopamine, which in turn makes him even more active and inclined to take risks, such as climbing on the furniture or throwing himself about in the flat. It is a wonder that he has developed such good language skills when he doesn't appear to hear most of what his family say to him at these times!

Despite his irritatingly active nature, Leroy is very attached to all the members of his overwhelmingly female family, and he demonstrates all the features of a child with secure attachment resulting from attention and affection. John Bowlby worked for many years to establish the importance of early attachment in building the foundations for successful relationships later in childhood. In 1956 he said: 'The children who in their school years and later are characterized by an excessive need for dependent relations and for attention and affection are in many cases the children who, during their first three years of life, have either not had the opportunity of making a satisfactory attachment or whose attachment, once made, has been stormy.' John Bowlby, 'The growth of independence in the young child', *Royal Society of Health Journal*, 76, pp 587-591, 1956)

Leroy's life chances have given him a secure attachment within a caring family, and this will stand him in good stead for the rest of his life. His extended family have always demonstrated great affection to each other and particularly to Leroy as the only boy in the family. This has not meant babying, indulging or feminising him, but being consistently affectionate, and having high but realistic expectations. Well attached children are more likely to have positive self esteem, make good relationships, be curious and confident, and have a highly developed sense of responsibility, all of which makes them better learners. Of course this is in direct opposition to some styles of parenting, where 'being independent and grown up' are expectations at an unrealistically early age, and may lead to insecurity and poor relationships later in life.

How much the chance of our nurture affects the way our brains develop is still open for discussion, but in Leroy's case, he seems to have had a lucky combination of nature, nurture and chance.

Key elements of the brain

High levels of testosterone in his brain make Leroy enthusiastic and well focused, and he has the added advantage that links between the two hemispheres of his brain have developed more quickly than in most boys, enabling him to use language as well as movement to motivate his friends and organise them in tasks. Most girls develop these language links earlier than most boys, so in this way, Leroy is rather unusual. He is already able to use the language of instruction, inspiration and organisation, and his ability to think quickly and turn this thinking into language will prove a great asset to him as a leader.

Many boys of Leroy's age will still be using the right hemisphere of their brains for language, combining words and movement, touching, knocking into, nudging and jostling their friends to show friendship and involvement or to attract their attention. Where Leroy's words come in sentences, many of his friends will still be using single words and short phrases in their play.

The balance of testosterone and oxytocin in Leroy's brain is such that although he is not very interested in sitting still for long periods, particularly when it is not an activity he has chosen himself, he *is* interested in language and talking to get what he wants and particularly to get other people on board with his plans. Oxytocin moderates the effects of testosterone, and the balance of these chemicals is vital in early language. Girls have the edge in speech and language due to their higher levels of oestrogen and oxytocin, which reinforces an interest in caring, in people and in language. Levels of oxytocin rise even higher when we talk to family and friends, making it a vital factor in good leadership.

However, the male brain adds something else to the mix. The production of dopamine, combined with testosterone result in an active body, impulsive behaviour and more 'doing', which Leroy demonstrates every day. He is very much a boy in this respect, needing to be active for most of the day, finding sedentary activities frustrating, and needing a good outside environment where he can deploy all his energy. The mixture of action and language is a magical component of Leroy's personality and part of his appeal to other boys is that he can put their plans into words and thus make them happen!

Leroy has a less extreme position on the gender spectrum than Paul, Adam or Donovan. He is active and lively, but his early language development may mean that he is nearer to the middle of the gender spectrum, a more even mix of masculine and feminine characteristics, and this will help him as he embarks on the early stages of education. Investigation of the structure of his brain would probably uncover these features:

- Leroy's language ability is almost certainly unusual among his peer group and in the area where he lives. This will be a distinct advantage in nursery and beyond, but it is important to remember that a skill that may be more unusual for a boy does not mean that the whole of Leroy's brain is more similar to that of a girl. It could be that Leroy's active nature results in less time for talk than most girls, and that unreasonable expectations may make him shut down.

- Better than usual language skills, combined with good attachment and an interest in people, will probably mean that Leroy may have good listening skills as well. Boys have growth spurts, which can affect their ear canals as well as their brains, leading to significant hearing loss. Hearing difficulties are more common in boys and 70% of boys of school age have poorer hearing than their female peers. Practitioners will need to observe him and his responses to instructions and conversations, and investigate any consistencies in what they observe.

- Because Leroy has good social and language skills, there may be a temptation to think he doesn't need as much active learning as other boys. This would be a huge mistake. He needs the action to help him formulate his ideas and plans. Problem solving for Leroy is inextricably linked with action. He talks about action, in action and through action. Watching his body as he talks and manages his group will reveal constant movement, gesture and facial expression. Making him sit still to talk will result in 'body and brain freeze', a feature of retreat into the primitive brain.

- Early spoken language doesn't necessarily mean early interest in writing or a desire to work or play with girls! Leroy's unique combination of 'clevernesses' still ties him securely to a male 'pack', and verbal ability does not mean readiness to write. Leroy will write for a purpose as he did in the story, but his reluctance to join adult directed mark-making and other literacy activities is a real indicator of his maleness.

- Sitting still and listening are still difficult for Leroy. The testosterone in his body, and a strong body structure inherited from both his parents will result in a restless disposition and a need for active learning with lots of physical challenges. Unlike Adam, his experiments are carried out on a large scale.

- Single mindedness and a drive to solve problems can be a difficult and frustrating combination for the adults who live and work with Leroy. Once he gets an idea in his head he is both tenacious and unstoppable, mobilising his troops to work with him, as they are always willing to do. Life for the troops is exciting and fulfilling. Being well managed is rewarding for them as well as for Leroy. For the adults such concerted action may derail their careful plans or at least make them quick thinkers too!

- Without a brain scan we don't know whether Leroy is using both sides of his brain for language. He may not be using the corpus callosum (the superhighway linking the two halves of the brain) he might just be enriching the right side of his brain: '...the nerve cells reaching across from the right cannot find a place to plug in. So they go back to the right side where they came from and plug in there instead. As a result, the right side of a boy's brain is richer in internal connections but poorer in cross connections to the other half'. Steve Biddulph, *Raising Boys* (Thorsons 2003)

The practitioners in Leroy's setting will need to be aware of the complexity of his brain and behaviour. They will need to be patient, understanding, quick thinkers, ready to respond to his sudden interests and projects and sensitive to the complexity of his learning. His parents, grandmothers and sisters have learned to manage this complexity with love and understanding. Now the school will need to build on this in ways that don't destroy his emerging 'clevernesses' of language and leadership.

Other influences

At home Leroy is supported by a range of nurturing styles, from his parents, often either his mum or his dad, depending on shifts; his twin sisters who alternate between treating him like a baby, involving him in complicated games, and shouting at his constant activity; and his grandmothers' unconditional love. On summer evenings he sometimes escapes to the park when the duty grandma will accompany him to sit nearby in the evening sun. His parents will sometimes spend a rare complete day taking all three children to a theme park or science museum.

Life in Leroy's home is not always consistent or predictable but it is bound together by love and care for each other. This will stand him in good stead as he progresses through school, and he is indeed fortunate; his life chances have dealt him a powerful hand in the game of life.

When he started in the nursery, there was a tendency to compare Leroy with his twin sisters, who were seven at the time he was admitted. The twins were well known, not just for their uncanny likeness to each other, but for their quiet and studious approach to school. Leroy was a bit of a surprise when he arrived, with his fascinating mixture of 'clevernesses'. It took some time to get to grips with him, without suppressing his spirit or being enchanted into indulgence by his behaviours and open approach.

Now it is up to the adults in Leroy's school to ensure they build on his strengths and help him to expand his interests to some of the things which are currently not high on his agenda, without stifling his ability to lead and inspire others, including his teachers. He will need to be motivated, challenged and engaged through active learning and a curriculum which includes an outdoor element and plenty of interesting problems to solve.

How to recognise and value the strengths of boys like Leroy

Some of the strategies that were discussed and implemented in reception and in the primary years to follow were:

- Boys like Leroy need to balance their obvious leadership within the group with involvement in adult-led activities and learning the skills they will need to succeed in school and in life. However, we must remember that: 'Adult-led activities are those which adults initiate. The activities are not play, and children are likely not to see them as play, but they should be playful – with activities presented to children which are as open-ended as possible, with elements of imagination and active exploration that will increase the interest and motivation for children.' *Learning, Playing and Interacting – Good Practice in the Early Years Foundation Stage* (DCSF 2009)
  - Make adult-led activities fun and collaborative, by setting challenges for groups of children and linking these to curriculum objectives set in a problem solving context. Begin to encourage children to use the library for information. Children are always keen to get involved in retrieving information from the internet and other electronic sources, so supervised access to these will motivate groups and individuals. Be a 'playful adult'.
  - Use the resources and equipment that boys are attracted to in more directed activities. As in Adam and Paul's settings, practitioners and teachers now plan for some of the adult-led activities to take place out of doors, using the resources and equipment that seem to motivate boys. Large construction with found materials, gardening, den-building and physical activity all lend themselves to group learning.
  - Tempt them into writing, reading, recording and calculating by providing plenty of writing and mark-making materials, and leaving some of these in outdoor areas or near the activities that Leroy and his friends use. Clipboards, pens, small whiteboards, small pads of paper, chalk, big felt-tipped pens, hand sprays and paint brushes will all encourage the making of marks and the development of hand and finger muscles needed for writing.

- Leroy needs to learn to channel his high levels of energy, without destroying the joy it gives him. Remember that 'Joy stimulates the temporal lobe and learning' Michael Gurian, *The Minds of Boys*, (Jossey Bass 2005) and that Leroy needs to maintain his joy in learning and language:

- Short bursts of fine motor skill will be more likely to motivate him than long periods of sitting still. A mixture of short bursts of attention to you and long periods of play, with you on hand as a resource, will be more effective. He will remember more of what you teach him if he has time to practise the skills in play.

- Give Leroy, and children like him, plenty of interesting materials and equipment to use both indoors and outside. Digital cameras, video recorders, metal detectors, big logs and stones to shift, poles, canes and tape for den-building will all encourage purposeful activities. When Leroy's school orders new outdoor equipment they always favour wheeled toys that can be used by more than one child at a time. 'The freedom to combine resources in many different ways may be especially important for flexible cognitive development, by enabling children to build pathways for thinking and learning, and to make connections across areas of experience.' *Learning, Playing and Interacting – Good Practice in the Early Years Foundation Stage* (DCSF 2009)

- Give time and an early warning of the end of periods of self-chosen activity, for 'transition time'. This will help active boys to bring their activities to a comfortable end. This will reduce stress and frustration, and the tears and tantrums that can result from sudden transitions.

- The school maintains a list of local groups for children in the community. Leroy's somewhat sheltered upbringing within his family could now be expanded by joining some community groups, and the local 'Lads and Dads' group proved to be just the thing to encourage his dad to make real efforts to be around for meetings where he could enjoy physical tasks and community projects with Leroy and other families. As Leroy moves up through the school, he could also be encouraged to join active after-school activities, to engage his enthusiasm and his energy. The school already provides a range of these for him to choose from.

- Leroy's need to lead may be stifling the independence of some other children:
  - Encourage Leroy to work in mixed groups with girls and the less active boys, by reorganising self-chosen groups for some activities, giving children an opportunity to get to know others in the group. Some of the quieter, less vocal boys (and some of the girls) will love to be included in

activities with Leroy, and they may well begin to expand his interests by introducing interests of their own and extending and refining his language.

Children like Leroy are a joy to have in any setting or school. Enthusiasm, interesting language and the ability to organise themselves and others is a rare combination in younger children and particularly in boys. As Leroy moves up through his primary years, he will continue to provide leadership and joy both to his friends and to the adults who work with him. His family continue to guide his efforts; activities with his father at the 'Lads and Dads' group have cemented the bond between father and son.

It is even giving his mum the model she needs to get involved in local community groups and make friends outside the family. Her confidence and ability to communicate in English have improved and she feels much more able to help all three of her children to remain motivated and successful at school. The grandmothers now attend the day room of the residential home where Leroy's mum works, and are having the time of their lives keeping their brains young in the wide range of activities provided there.

Michael the superhero

Michael's story

Most of what I know and understand about superheroes I learned from Michael! His knowledge was second to none. It didn't matter whether it was Spiderman, Superman, Batman or Ninja Turtles, there was almost nothing Michael didn't know about them. Most of the other boys in my class were pretty good, but when Michael arrived on the scene he became the uncontested expert. He had only been with us a few short weeks, and as he was in foster care, we weren't entirely sure how long he'd be with us for, but he was certainly keeping us all on our toes in the superhero department!

So besotted with them was Michael that he could ingeniously turn any activity into a superhero extravaganza! In the painting area he painted superheroes. In the construction area he built sets for them and in the workshop area he made superhero masks and costumes. When it came to imaginative play, either indoors or outside Michael could be found directing extended superhero role-plays. It was an interesting time, not least because it forced our team, which was 80 per cent female to take a long hard look at superhero play. There was no doubt about it; superhero play was Michael's salvation. In spite of a sad personal history, he was an extremely lively and happy four year old. His superhero friends occupied all of his waking moments, and as his foster mother commented one morning when she bought him into school, 'I'm sure Michael plays Ninja Turtles in his sleep – you should have seen the state of his bed this morning!'.

'Yes, he does rather love his superheroes doesn't he' I said.

'You're not kidding!' she replied. 'Still, I mustn't grumble, he's a great little lad and no trouble to have around at all, except I swear I'll need a new sofa in the near future. Mine's not built to withstand quite so many superheroes bouncing on it!'

'Oh dear,' I said sympathetically. 'Yes, I have noticed that as far as Michael's concerned its superheroes any time, any place and anywhere!'

And this was just the problem, though I didn't admit to Michael's foster mum that his particular type of play was causing some of us a few headaches! Whether dressed up or not, Michael went everywhere at the speed of light, wielding his various weapons as he went. If he wasn't saving the planet he was capturing baddies and consigning them to dungeons where they would remain for the rest of their lives until they died in misery! He 'zapped' everything that moved (and some things that didn't) and once climbed fearlessly up on top of the bike store while in the process of spinning a web! Some of the girls were terrified of him, especially when he rampaged round the outside area on a bike, cloak flowing behind him zapping everything in sight! He was never happier than when dressed up as one of his heroes, and if he didn't get to the dressing area in enough time to 'bags' the costume he wanted he would make do with his coat – worn only by the hood!

What was it we asked ourselves that made these characters so appealing to small boys, especially vulnerable young boys like Michael? I remember we spent much time reflecting on this question at our review meetings. Certainly there seemed to be something around power. Superheroes can sort out problems with the swipe of a laser or the skilful use of a morpher, and this must be very attractive to a vulnerable young child! There was also something around strength, speed, scary situations, rescue and the unadulterated flashy appearance of these superhero idols. Clearly Michael, and others like him, derived huge benefits from such play. In fact, in Michael's case I was convinced it was positively therapeutic. I had observed him carefully, and although he was essentially a happy little boy his troubled background had taken its toll. When he wasn't playing superheroes I had often noticed him idly staring into space, and it was at these times that the pain of his particular circumstances could be seen in his face. Not so when he was playing. Any sense of pain disappeared and his expression became relaxed and full of joy as any stress or anguish simply dropped away. Indeed, whatever issues this play was giving us were ours and not his, and they needed to be sorted out!

As I stood musing on this point I heard a blood-curdling scream emanating from the home corner, so without stopping to think further, I hurried to the scene to investigate. I was met by an enraged Mimi, who informed me in no uncertain terms that the commotion was all the fault of the boys!

'It's them lot!' she shrieked, pointing an accusing finger at three boys dressed in various superhero costumes. Michael stood in the middle in a Spiderman costume looking positively affronted.

'We ain't done nothing,' he protested. 'We was just trying to get the blanket off the bed. We need it to rescue someone – they need to jump into it to escape from the Cybermen.'

'Yeah well, you could at least have asked before you took it and you shouldn't have pushed Tatiana and made her bump her head. Anyway, you can't have it 'cause we need it!' continued Mimi. Tatiana, who was standing to the side of Mimi with Lucy's protective arm around her, now decided to join the fray! 'And they was jumping off the windowsill on to the bed, and that's not what the bed's for and they shouldn't be doing that in the home corner where us lot am playing!'

I couldn't help but agree, although I secretly hoped that I would be able to communicate this in a slightly less sanctimonious way.

'Well it's alright for you to say that,' said Michael, looking extremely wronged. 'We're just trying to save the world!'

'I understand that,' I said, trying to take account of everyone's point of view. 'However, I don't think the home corner is quite the place for doing it.'

'Well where can we do it then?' asked Michael, with mounting frustration. 'We already tried doing it in the soft play and Miss Davies told us to go away.'

'Yeah, and then we went outside and Mrs Marshall told us to stop before we made someone fall off a bike!' added Delroy.

It was at this point that I decided that we must sort this out at our next review meeting.

'I tell you what,' I said. 'Just for now go and play saving the world on the grass behind the shed.' (This was usually out of bounds as it was very near to a Key Stage 2 classroom, but as the class in question were out on a visit I thought it would be alright.) 'And if you go into the book corner you can borrow the red blanket from in there.'

'Wow, thanks!' chorused the boys, who disappeared in a flash. 'Walk to the book corner!' I shouted, without effect.

As I turned to look at the girls I noticed that they looked somewhat victorious, and with the superheroes dispatched to the outside area they soon resumed their play.

Later that day, our team sat down to discuss proceedings. We had always had superhero play, but since Michael had joined us it had gathered an unprecedented momentum, and the situation needed addressing with some urgency. As usual, the team were full of helpful positive suggestions.

'It wasn't a problem before, but now that so many of the boys are into this type of play it's getting a bit of an issue,' said Maureen.

'Yes,' agreed Sue. 'It's not that they're doing anything wrong. It's just that they're so lively that it's interfering with everyone else's play and if we're not careful someone's going to get hurt.'

'Well the answer seems simple enough,' said Lynn. 'Why don't we designate the area next to the wild garden a superhero zone? There's enough space and we can explain it to everyone at circle time tomorrow. That way they can play superheroes to their hearts' content without getting in anyone else's way!'

'Brilliant!' I said, and 'The Zone' was born.

In the weeks that followed 'The Zone' became a most popular and productive place, and a place where Michael spent much of his time. As the primary user of this new resource he became its unofficial custodian, and I remember how one day, aggravated by the behaviour of some 'new' boys to the area, he strode towards me, red in the face and said, 'We need some rules for 'The Zone' cause some kids is coming in there and being a pain!'

'OK!' I said. 'We'll do it at small group time.' What followed was a brainstorming session where the children generated clear guidelines for keeping play safe. At Michael's instigation these were written up, laminated and displayed in 'The Zone'.

We did not allow toy weapons in the setting, although if the children wanted to make weapons for use in 'The Zone' they could make them from the range of open-ended materials in the workshop area, and this they did in abundance. They also made masks, wristbands, capes, and all other manner of superhero paraphernalia. Their narratives were becoming more and more complex and several of us worked with the children to support them to photograph their stories and turn them into books and Powerpoint displays. 'The Zone' also sported magnificent superhero number lines and alphabets. We noticed how much the children's social skills developed as they worked their way around conflicts and disagreements about who should play what with whom. Everything in 'The Zone' revolved around superheroes and if you ever needed to find Michael you never had far to look. He was in his element.

I must admit that the girls seldom went to 'The Zone'. I once remember when one of the boys attempted some 'shooting' in the graphics area he was told emphatically by Tatiana to 'GO TO THE ZONE!'

'What's The Zone?' asked a visitor to our unit, with interest.

'It's where you have to go if you want to shoot people,' replied Tatiana. 'It's outside.'

Our visitor probed a little more. 'Do you go to The Zone?' she asked, at which point Mimi piped in.

'No! We only go there if Omar's there 'cause Tatiana loves him.' Mimi stifled a giggle.

'No I don't you little liar,' protested Tatiana. 'I'll show you where it is if you like,' she continued in an attempt to deflect the conversation away from Omar.

The lady was escorted to 'The Zone' where Michael gave her a guided tour and a full explanation of its purpose and its rules. I remember this day vividly as it was part way through this process that Michael's social worker pulled into the school car park. Within a few minutes she appeared in the company of the headteacher and explained that it would be necessary for her to take

Michael with her without delay. I remember being a little shocked but went over to Michael to explain. He was wearing his favourite Spiderman costume and I suspect would have protested loudly about having to leave had I not agreed to him leaving his costume on.

During the days that followed we did not see Michael, and as it transpired, we never saw him again. Apparently, for reasons of child protection it had become necessary to move him to another foster home. Everyone was very sad, especially when, several weeks later we received a package containing the Spiderman suit. We all thought about Michael often and sincerely hoped that wherever he was he was happy and had access to a place called THE ZONE!

How Michael's brain affects his behaviour

Superhero Michael is a fascinating mixture of vulnerability and strength, activity and stillness, and it is easy to understand some of the causes of what might be happening in his brain, and to mourn the chances that will certainly have altered its structure and functioning. However, there are also factors working to protect Michael's equilibrium in the face of constant disruption and change, and we can explore some of them here.

If you saw Michael when he was born you might not predict that his future would be so turbulent. His mother, although young, was healthy and well nourished. She had followed a normal pregnancy, apart from being a smoker, which may have put Michael at the lower end of the normal birth weight range for a boy. His father was present when he was born, and at the time, held a good job, providing a comfortable living for the family.

What you might not have known was that he was already at high risk of experiencing a disrupted and possibly damaging childhood. In Leroy's story we explored the place of attachment in enabling children to become confident and enthusiastic learners. Michael is not as lucky as Leroy. Soon after his birth, his dad lost his job and took off one night, never to be heard of again. His mother fell into a deep post-natal depression, and Michael's maternal grandfather took them to live at his house, trying his best to understand what his daughter was experiencing, and making a good attempt at remembering what bringing up a baby entailed. However, this didn't last long; eventually he began to lose patience and became increasingly stressed, both by his daughter's inability to 'pull herself together' and by Michael's long periods of distressed crying with colic.

Babies need close contact with their mothers, and there is now evidence that the activity of breastfeeding, which brings the baby's vision in focus with his/her mother's face is a vital component of attachment, and of healthy cognitive development. Secure attachment develops when babies are held, and a two-month-old baby is deemed to need to be held for at least two hours in every 24. Michael's mum found it difficult to even be aware of him. She did not breastfeed, and his grandfather took over the bottle feeding, often as he watched television or read the paper, failing to make the vital eye-contact Michael needed for brain growth and attachment. Michael responded to this treatment by wriggling and refusing the bottle to continue his crying. No-one thought to question whether the formula in Michael's bottle was the cause, or the lack of attention.

'Boys seek and hold eye contact less than girls, and are consequently less likely to be picked up or held for longer.' Michael Gurian, *The Minds of Boys* (Jossey Bass 2005)

As a result, Michael was not only under-nourished, he was 'unattached'. His brain was suffering from lack of nutrients, particularly the high fat content of breast milk, which is vital in building links between brain cells, creating a strong immune system and reinforcing learning. He was also learning very quickly that he was unimportant and that his mother was not interested in him. The stress of separation at such an early age has a lasting effect on brain development, encouraging the growth of the parts of the brain that deal with anxiety and fear, and leaving the thinking brain, the limbic system (the emotional part of the brain) and the hippocampus (the part of the brain which processes long-term memory) underdeveloped. The result of this stress in very young and abused children is to leave them with a reduced ability to think logically and make relationships, and increased levels of anxiety, fear and instability.

Despite support from a health visitor and the family GP, Michael's situation deteriorated until social workers stepped in and made a decision to take him into care when he was 13 months, placing him in a series of short-term foster placements, where he stayed until we met him.

Of course, the legislation in England regarding children in the care of the local authority (now referred to as Looked After Children) has changed since Michael entered nursery, but no legislation can make a mother love a baby. The Children Act and its associated legislation and guidance are intended to improve the situations of children whose parents are not able to look after them, however, even this new legislation has not been without its troubling cases and statistics. As *The Guardian* newspaper reported in April 2009, Michael is one of the 60,000 children currently in the care of local authorities, and: 'More than 1,000 children have been placed with at least 10 different families, while 10 children moved through at least 50 homes as local authorities failed to find them a permanent placement. The quality of foster care across the country has raised serious concern and there is growing unease about the low level of training and qualifications required of workers in residential care homes.' Amelia Gentleman, *The Guardian* (Monday 20 April 2009) Michael is one of these children.

Key elements of the brain

The unique structure of Michael's brain makes him vulnerable, but his brain has also developed systems and strategies for protecting him from the world. His levels of testosterone are high, and stress chemicals including cortisol in his body and brain top up the fuel for action and movement. He reacts to stressful events by becoming a superhero, or withdrawing into himself, sometimes frozen in thought or memory. These are classic behaviours of a child's reaction moving past the amygdala, the gateway to the more primitive part of the brain, into parts of the brain where reactions are simple – 'flight' (withdrawal), 'fight' (in superhero mode) or 'freeze'.

His superhero fixation is partly due to testosterone levels, but it is also a mechanism for survival. Superheroes are invincible, they rescue people and have special powers such as the ability to fly or climb high buildings. They can destroy enemies with a wave of the hand or even a look! How attractive this must be to a small vulnerable boy, who feels powerless to control his own life. The strong colours (dark blue, red, deep green, black) are very attractive to boys, stimulating movement, action, anger, power and hunger in the brain. Dressed in a superhero cloak, Michael is ready to conquer the world. No wonder he sometimes needs to wear it all day, and it is a lifeline as he moves on to the next foster home, and the next school. A worrying factor for his future is the return through the post of his superhero cloak with no note, which might indicate a less accommodating environment.

Michael needs to manage his environment and the people within it. With reduced feelings of attachment, the knowledge that his stay will probably be temporary, and a brain distracted by anxiety, he needs to feel in control, and the superhero persona will allow him to do so, at least with the boys. He needs the support of understanding adults to mediate on his behalf, and a programme that presents him with plenty of opportunities to succeed. Failure is familiar, success and praise are rare and he treats them with distrust, so practitioners need to proceed with care.

Throughout his short life, apart from when he adopts his alternative persona as a superhero, Michael has also been a listener and watcher, the direct opposite of his 'speeding arrow' superhero mode. This ability to stay still and listen has helped his language development and made his hearing acute.

He has a lot of experience of listening to adult conversations through walls and from the top of the stairs, and of making what sense he can of what he hears. He has learned to keep quiet at home, sometimes in the hope of becoming part of a good experience, sometimes to avoid the worst excesses of poorer foster care placements where other children teased and even bullied him.

However, there is something indestructible about Michael's spirit. He always seems able to 'give it another go' when he arrives in a new setting. The new start with new friends and equipment always manages to inspire him, and this spirit endears him to adults and other children, who readily include him in their play. His small stature and ready smile reduce any threat to existing friendships, although the boys usually place him pretty low in the pecking order of the pack! Once he is in his costume, even if it is only the hood of his coat, he can face anything, he will often remain in these clothes all day, whatever he is doing, and wise practitioners will allow this.

It is difficult to place Michael accurately on the gender spectrum. He is definitely very masculine in his behaviour, but his vulnerability and sensitivity give him some more feminine characteristics. His behaviour swings from ebullience to vulnerability, and this is probably a result of the chance experiences of his short life. His 'clevernesses' are many and some of them are unusual in such a young child:

- Michael's limbic system (the emotional part of his brain) can trigger him to fade into the background, particularly if he feels threatened or is asked to do something he can't yet do. This behaviour is often missed by adults, who notice him and engage with him more when he is active, but it is a survival technique which protects him and comforts him, leaving him unnoticed to observe what is happening and allowing him to follow the lead of other children.

- He is very resilient and adaptable (at least on the surface). A child with less resilience might have collapsed completely into depression, silence or violent behaviour, each of which has long-term implications. This resilience will also stand him in good stead, because his life will continue to throw new chances at him.

- Michael is able to remove himself from the pain and difficulty of his early life by absorbing himself in a story where he is strong, powerful and can destroy those who might hurt him. This ability to withdraw into fantasy will protect him in his early years, but may prove a difficulty for him as he grows up and fantasy is a more risky occupation. Creative fantasy play often develops into creative thinking at a later age, but it does need to be inspired by resources, places and language, and particularly the company of thoughtful, responsive adults, who can: 'Scaffold children's learning through talk, discussing strategies and ideas, suggesting possibilities and modelling approaches'. *Learning, Playing and Interacting: Good Practice in the Early Years Foundation Stage* (DCSF 2009)

- Michael also has an unusual pattern of language development – acute powers of hearing and a facility to 'parrot' the adult language he hears but does not always understand. This is not always appreciated by adults. Much of his language when he is in superhero mode is very typical of boys of his age, speaking or shouting in single words or short phrases like 'C'mon', 'Let's go!', 'Up here', 'You dead'. This shorthand is called 'text speak' by Anne Moir in *Brain Sex* (Dell Publishing 1992): 'Language development is slower in boys, and many parents will observe that they use sounds, such as motor noises, far more than actual words. In their developing speech, nearly all of the sounds little girls make tend to be verbally communicative, whereas with boys only something like 40 per cent are verbal; the rest is just noises.' Ian Grant, *Growing Great Boys* (Vermillion 2008)

- Michael's teacher discovered a real 'cleverness' in Michael, sadly, just before he left the nursery. Like some other children who have been abused, Michael is fascinated with numbers, counting and calculating, shapes and space, money and measuring. Maybe this fascination is linked to the certainty and logic of maths, or perhaps he is genetically pre-disposed to become a mathematician. The sad chance of his life means that his teacher never knew where Michael went – and had no way of telling his next teacher about it.

Children like Michael continue to be at risk in our communities and our schools: 'Children in the care of LAs are one of the most vulnerable groups in society. The majority of children who remain in care are there because they have suffered abuse or neglect. At any one time around 60,000 children are looked after in England, although some 90,000 pass through the care system in any year.' Royal College of Psychiatrists, 'Mental health and growing up, 3rd edition: Domestic violence: Its effects on children', (2004)

Other influences

Colic in early childhood, and the interrupted sleep patterns that it induced, have been a feature of Michael's life. Extreme wakefulness was the reason for transfer from two of his foster placements. Michael has always been a fussy eater, and this started when he was a baby. He still likes soft, undemanding food, and refuses most fruit and vegetables. His weight, his teeth and his general health are all at long-term risk, and no-one has been with him long enough to help him tackle these problems. Even his enormous energy could be a problem, depleting reserves in his small frame, and presenting a challenge to every foster placement and setting he attends.

Determination is a character trait everyone associates with Michael and admires in him. He is determinedly resilient, taking everything life offers him in his stride, and this is a real strength as he copes with constant change. However, he is just as determined about 'I can't go to sleep', 'I 'ates carrots', 'I really *need* to wear the Batman cloak to assembly!' or 'My granddad *is* coming today'.

Being enrolled at a day care setting when he was two increased his feelings of insecurity and this brought on bedwetting and tantrums. Although his key person at the setting and his foster mother talked in detail about how to get over these issues, they found no solution and the situation remained unresolved as the foster family moved to Scotland and Michael was once again moved within the local authority, to avoid 'out of area' payments for his care. The guidance for placements out-of-authority are now much clearer, ensuring that information is shared and there is a balance between keeping children within foster families, and moving them away from their natural parents and locality.

The only solid support in Michael's young life is the continuing presence of his grandfather, who will turn up at the foster placement (usually unannounced) to offer a small gift or toy, and spend a few precious minutes with him. No-one knows where his grandfather lives, and he has lost touch with Michael's mother, but he does keep in contact with the social worker to find out where Michael is. He remembers his birthday and Christmas and has given him a photo of the three generations of his family (his parents, grandfather and Michael), taken soon after he was born. Needless to say, this photo is Michael's most treasured possession!

How to recognise and value the strengths of boys like Michael

National Statistics tell us that more boys than girls are now looked after by local authorities (what was previously termed 'In Care') and this number is increasing every year. Many of these boys go on to have mental health disorders, fail to reach their potential at school, are unemployed or involved in crime. How can we help Michael and children like him, when we may only have days or weeks to make a difference before they move on?

- Providing a secure environment is a key feature for boys like Michael. However long he stays, and whatever his difficulties, he needs to feel both safe and secure in nursery and at school. His desire for affection, close attachment and admiration are all features of his needs, and some settings would feel reluctant to put effort into making a difference for him or accepting his behaviours and priorities. Fortunately, this nursery is one where every effort is made to include new children, to help them gain entry into existing groups, and to make every day or week a good one.
  - Greet every child by name early on in every day. This is very important to all children, particularly boys. Girls will usually seek out adults to talk to, boys may not do so.
  - Provide not just safety and acceptance, but clear expectations. All boys, and insecure boys in particular, really need rules. They may seem to be testing these all the time, but that is just what it is – testing to make sure they know clearly who is in charge, who cares about their safety, about fairness, about behaviour. Michael really needed those rules about The Zone, and it is important to him to have his views taken seriously.

- Michael needs to feel that his major play interests are appreciated and supported. Superheroes are very important to him. He responds well to a setting where superheroes are accepted and managed, not banned.
  - Staff should discuss their approach to superhero play and make sure their response is unified. Read *We don't Play with Guns Here*, by Penny Holland (Open University Press 2003), or *Boys and Girls; Superheroes in the Doll Corner*, by Vivian Gussin Paley (Chicago University Press 1986), which explore the issues of superhero play in nursery classes. These books, written by practitioners, will inform your discussions and give you ideas for strategies.

    Develop some problem-solving approaches and make time to discuss the issues of gun play or superhero play with the children. Children live in an increasingly violent society, where world events of violence are routinely broadcast before the watershed. Video and DVD watching in our homes is often unrestricted, and children are watching material that they would never have seen a generation ago. Ignoring this won't make it go away!

    '25% of under twos have a TV in their bedroom, and two-thirds of pre-school boys spend more than two hours looking at screens which is three times the time they spend with books or being read to.' Michael Gurian, *The Minds of Boys* (Jossey Bass 2005)
  - Use replica figures of superheroes and TV or film characters for small-world play in sand, water, construction and story-telling. These will often

spark more interest than the more traditional education-based figures. Take photos of these figures and use them for PowerPoint presentations or photo-books. Boys will often be inspired to write and tell stories though these activities.

- The setting in the story developed a strategy for dealing with superhero play – 'The Zone'. Is there a place in your setting for an area where groups of children can play out their anxieties and stories? Develop and agree rules for these areas, knowing that all children, and boys in particular, need rules and boundaries.

- Michael's arrival at the nursery was as sudden and unexpected as his departure. Researchers, watching children in early years settings, have noted that boys have a tendency to ignore newcomers, whereas girls tend to welcome them and include them in their play. How do you help the children in your group to accept newcomers when they arrive after planned induction or unexpectedly?
  - Stories and discussions can help to prepare children for all sorts of unexpected events see page 126 for some suggested titles. Make sure you have some of these stories available, and don't just tell them after the child arrives!
  - If there is a problem, get used to discussing it with the children and asking for their solutions. You will be surprised how willing they are to make suggestions, both for rules and sanctions – in fact you may have to tone down some of their ideas for punishments!

- New children need time to settle in, to make acquaintances, to find their feet. Some of the strategies that settings have adopted are:
  - Buddying or pairing of a new child with a confident member of the existing group sometimes helps both sides when introducing a new member of the class. Choose a child who will take the role seriously and genuinely use their position to ease the way.
  - Amend your programme for the first few days, make more space for play and building friendships, make more time for adults to be free to support and get to know the new child and their foster family.
  - If the child is confident, let them talk to their key person, key group or even the whole group about what they like doing at nursery. However, avoid putting them in a difficult position in talking about their problems and the reasons for their differences.

- Adult support is important to Michael and boys like him, but he may not let you know this, or even be aware of it himself. Adults have let him down all through his life, and even those he thought he could trust, such as some of the foster carers, practitioners at previous settings, and even his grandfather have failed to prevent the constant moves and disruptions to his life. It will take sympathetic and sensitive adult support, lots of patient listening and talking to get him to trust adults and let them in. But practitioners in the early years are persistent and professional, and we can only hope that Michael may stop long enough in the next placement for one of them to make a relationship with him. Other children with the same issues might be helped by some of the following strategies:

- Use stories about other children facing problems like theirs (see page 126 for suggested titles), and provide opportunities to talk about them in small groups and sessions where everyone feels safe and free to talk or remain silent.
- All children, and particularly boys need help in talking about feelings. Use your own or other available support materials such as the SEAL programme, puppets or Persona Dolls to explore situations such as loneliness, bullying, shyness and so on. Don't just focus on one thing or the problems of one child. Discuss a range of situations.
- Use all the opportunities that arise to help children to discuss and accept differences by using books, songs, small-world figures, drama and role-play. Make sure that parents and foster parents of vulnerable children have contacts for out-of-school activities such as Shine, or the National Reading Campaign, where sport is used as a way to get boys and their dads involved in reading together.
- Children like Michael would now have a pre-school Personal Education Plan (PEP) outlining his individual needs, a teacher within the setting responsible for his welfare, and an inspection system which is intended to ensure quality at all levels. You can find out about this at: www.dcsf.gov.uk/everychildmatters/safeguardingandsocialcare/childrenincare.

Children like Michael may under-achieve throughout the education system, and some spend their lives in a desperate search for acceptance and love. They often make miscalculations as they put new friends or partners on a pedestal before realising that they are just human! However, other children who have been neglected in the way Michael was are lucky enough to make secure attachments, find fulfilment in their interests and make good parents themselves, committed to providing a better life for their children.

We must hope that Michael is one of these, and work to improve the situation for children like him.

Oliver the thinker

Oliver's story

'Quick!' yelled Oliver at the top of his voice. 'Everybody come and look at this. There's two massive enormous footprints in the garden – and they've got to be dragon prints – I just know they are!' In an instant there was a trail of children behind Oliver, all anxious to see the object of this intriguing revelation. By the time I got there Oliver was in full flow. 'Look everybody, there's two sets of footprints so that means that two dragons have been in the garden – probably last night when we weren't here – and look, there's loads of apple cores all over the place, and dragons like to eat apples so I bet they dropped them when they were here. I don't know why they came. Perhaps they wanted something, or maybe they wanted to give us something. I don't know, but it's very interesting.'

I watched to see what would happen next. Clearly, there were some children who shared Oliver's interest in the mysterious footprints, but once the initial viewing was over, the more disinterested among the group drifted back to what they obviously considered more worthwhile pursuits. As for Oliver, this discovery was to hold his interest for several days. Oliver was a thinker; always asking questions and questioning everything. He was also incredibly persistent and when driven by his insatiable curiosity to find answers to his questions, he kept us all on our toes. Add to this the fact that he was also extremely imaginative and you could be sure that life with Oliver would never be dull!

Sometimes Oliver could appear to be doing very little. You would see him, standing motionless, apparently lost in his own world, but we all knew, having worked with him for over a year, that far from doing nothing at such times, he was thinking deeply. Today, however, it was time for action. Oliver raced inside to fetch magnifying glasses. I smiled as I watched. He was short for his age and slightly tubby, but in his anxiety to return to the footprints, his legs were working uncharacteristically quickly. With a great sense of urgency, he distributed the magnifiers to the children who had remained. 'Now everyone, listen, if the dragons were here last night they might have dropped some scales, so everybody search and see if you can see one.' A hush descended around the muddy footprints as the children searched in earnest for dragon scales.

'What do they look like?' asked Joshua, becoming slightly de-motivated when a scale failed to jump out at him.

'Well,' explained Oliver, 'they're kind of hard and sparkly, a bit like glass.'

'How d'you know?' questioned Joshua, 'I bet you ain't never seen one!'

'I have in books,' replied Oliver, continuing to search.

'Look, here's one!' bellowed Sam triumphantly.

'Where?' asked Oliver, leaping over the mud to see.

Sam held up something green, which looked to me suspiciously like a piece of glass from an old beer bottle, rubbed smooth by years of being in the ground, but Oliver was convinced. 'It is one Sam – it's a scale – let's take it inside and put it safe.'

Just then the bell rang for tidy-up time, so any more scale-searching had to be abandoned for that day, but I knew that that was not the last we would hear of the dragons in the garden. Once the children had gone home, I reflected on the day, and wondered what had made the mysterious marks in the mud, for you had to admit, they did look very like the claw marks of a rather large creature.

The next morning, Oliver self-registered with extreme speed; such was his anxiety to get out into the garden to see if any more footprints had appeared. To his disappointment, they hadn't, but this was not to deter him from further investigations into possible dragon visitations.

As I looked outside I saw him hurrying towards the door with a plastic bucket full of assorted pieces of apple. 'Look,' he shrieked excitedly, 'I can't find any more footprints but the dragons have been here for sure 'cause they've left loads of bits of apple, and look, most of 'em have got teeth marks in! And that's not all – on the tree by the fence there's a whole load of claw marks – like as if the dragons have been trying to eat the leaves off the top of the trees. But best of all, look!' Oliver put down the bucket, dug into his pocket with a very dirty hand, and with a flourish, produced some gold coloured coins that looked like foreign currency. 'They've left some treasure, and I bet there's a load more and all.'

With this he went off to put his precious apples pieces and coins alongside his dragon scale. A little later I noticed he had left a message by his exhibits, which read 'plez do not tuch'. He then zoomed off to hunt for further treasure.

I was, therefore, slightly surprised when a short while later he reappeared requesting a plaster. Apparently, he had hurt his hand a few days earlier and some over-zealous digging had, as he put it 'knocked me scab off'. As I looked at his hand I had to smile. Only Oliver could take this opportunity to inform me about the purpose of a scab! 'If you cut yourself,' he explained, 'you have to have a plaster until you get a scab because scabs stop your blood coming out and if you haven't got a scab you need a plaster and I did have a scab but now it's all knocked off I'll have to have a plaster until I get a new scab you see.' I think I followed! We sorted out a plaster and Oliver was soon off again to resume his search.

I would have liked to have spent more time with Oliver that morning, but unfortunately, we were being monitored by a local authority inspector so it would have to wait until later. Mind you, Oliver was to provide further amusement that morning. The particular inspector in question was hovering around in search of a child who would like to talk to him. He had made several requests which had all met with refusals and it was just as he was being rebuffed yet again that Oliver appeared with another dragon scale to add to his exhibits. He approached the man with great enthusiasm and said, 'Would you like to talk to me about what I've been doing?'

'Oh, that would be lovely!' replied the inspector, blissfully unaware of what he was in for. To cut a long story short, an hour later he was attempting to back away from Oliver. 'Thank you, thank you Oliver,' he said, 'that was extremely interesting.'

'But I haven't finished yet!' replied Oliver, refusing to let the man go. I stifled a giggle at the sight of this man grappling unsuccessfully to extricate himself from the situation. Oliver was firmly in control and the inspector was still Oliver's captive audience when the bell went for tidy-up time. I think we can safely say that Oliver had unwittingly managed to sabotage the monitoring and I secretly hoped it didn't mean that our inspector would make a return visit.

Throughout the afternoon Oliver continued the search for treasure, and I was amazed when, just before snack time he came running in with a whole collection of things. 'Look at this lot!' he said as he laid his treasures out on the table. 'There's a gold necklace and some more coins and some precious stones. The dragons must have buried them in the sandpit 'cause that's where we found them. I reckon they're coming every single night to eat our apples and bury their treasure. If we collect it every day after they've been in the night we'll have loads and loads of stuff,' he said, extending his arms and puffing out his chest as if to emphasise the magnitude of his statement.

As Oliver pored over his treasure I was given to wonder just how all of these things had got into the sandpit. Perhaps they had been carried there from the dressing-up area by one of our little 'transporters,' or maybe one of the other groups had been having a treasure hunt. Either way, they had provided Oliver with much food for thought, in fact, even more so than I first predicted.

The next day when he arrived at school he was looking very thoughtful. 'Are you going to search for more treasure today Oliver?' I asked with interest. 'The dragons may have made another visit last night.'

'I don't think so,' he said with great certainty.

'Oh, why's that?' I enquired, 'I thought you were really interested in the dragons, and I've sorted out all these dragon books for you.'

'Well I am,' he explained, 'but I've been thinking about things and it doesn't seem right.'

'What doesn't seem right?' I went on to ask.

Oliver looked very serious. 'Well, all that treasure we've dug up isn't really ours is it?'

'What do you mean?' I said probing a little more.

'It belongs to the dragons doesn't it, and we've taken it and put it inside where they can't get it and they might have come back to look for it and thought that someone had stolen it, and it's not good to steal stuff is it?'

'Well no, it's not.' I agreed. 'So what do you think we should do about it?'

Oliver was resolute. 'I think we should give it back,' he said, 'we could leave it in the garden tonight and I think we should leave the dragons a present to say sorry for taking their treasure and we should write a letter to say sorry.'

I realised that this was a very serious moral dilemma for Oliver and tried to be supportive. 'Yes, we could do that,' I said. 'I could help you to write the letter and have you thought about what you might like to leave as a present?'

'Yes,' said Oliver, 'I've been reading in a dragon book. Dragons come from China and they like lanterns so I could make them a lantern.'

'That's a good idea,' I said, 'you could get everything ready today and we could put it out just before home time so that it will be ready for the dragons.'

Oliver worked with great seriousness that day and by home time everything was ready. Together we carried the treasure, Oliver's lavish lantern, the letter and for good luck, some apples into the garden. We laid them out underneath the climbing frame so they would not get wet if it rained, and then went back inside. 'I hope they come for their stuff,' said Oliver with a worried look in his eyes.

I tried to be reassuring. 'I think they will you know,' I said, making a mental note to ensure that I retrieved the things from beneath the climbing frame before going home. When the children had departed, I went to the staff room to collect some things I needed and was about to hurry back to my room when I overheard a conversation that captured my attention. We were a large unit, so staff didn't always get the opportunity to fully inform each other about everything that was happening.

'I don't know,' said Sue, one of the other staff, 'you think you know what will capture children's imaginations but you can never actually be sure. Do you know, two of my boys have really been into dragons so I set up a provocation. I made some footprints in the mud, left apples with teeth marks in them lying about and buried treasure, but it was all a waste of time because they never even noticed!'

I started to laugh. 'And what's amusing you?' asked Sue.

'Well now,' I began to explain, 'all that trouble you went to was certainly not wasted. For the last three days Oliver's had a wonderful time thinking about dragons'. When I had told her the rest of the story she smiled.

'Well that's great!' she said. 'It just goes to show that when you plan for one child's interests you may capture someone completely different. I agreed and went off to fetch the things from beneath the climbing frame. Needless to say, when Oliver arrived the next day he was overjoyed and relieved to find that the treasure was gone and that the dragons had accepted his peace offering with no ill will.

He stood for a moment looking thoughtful. Then he announced, 'I need to find a book about wizards'.

'I'll come and help you' I said, although I couldn't help wondering where that was going to lead us!

How Oliver's brain affects his behaviour

Oliver's brain is always in overdrive. Not the sort of overdrive that makes Donovan play football, or makes Paul rush about outdoors. Oliver's brain is always thinking, problem solving, following clues and trails in learning. When something puzzles him or looks different and intriguing, he responds by thinking. He makes predictions, joins up bits of information, talks to anyone who will listen, and becomes generally obsessed by the matter at hand. He is just the boy to respond to events or even the weather. He will become absorbed in smoke, clouds, ice, dripping taps, spilled paint, a bird's egg, a spider's web, or a 'thinking trap' set by a practitioner. In this case it was a trap set by a practitioner from another group, making the puzzle even more intriguing.

Practitioners in the early years have always been good at setting traps for learning, bringing objects to intrigue and interest children, sharing experiences, looking at natural objects and discussing 'What if...?'. We now know why this is an important part of learning, novelty engages the brain, and Oliver is a particularly good example of this. Because he is very observant and imaginative, he responds well, noticing when things are different, objects have been moved or conditions have changed. His imaginative nature then takes over and he makes up convincing reasons why things have happened, using his wide general knowledge, and, when this fails him, his imagination.

Oliver's genetic make-up will certainly have affected his learning styles and behaviours. His father is a technologist, currently working on new designs for wind turbines. His mother is a music teacher, who also writes and records songs for children. She works as a part-time music specialist in the primary part of the school where five-year-old Oliver attends the early years unit, currently in his reception year. He is one of the oldest children in the group, and his physical and intellectual development give evidence of his autumn birthday.

Oliver is the youngest of four brothers, being something of a surprise to his parents when he arrived six years after his youngest brother, and when his other brothers were ten and eight. All four brothers share an interest in the natural world and in music, and they have always been encouraged to think creatively.

Oliver is gregarious, but sometimes gets frustrated by the other children in the early years unit, who don't have his powers of concentration and sustained interest. They find him friendly but a bit pompous! His male brain gives him great powers of focus and concentration, and his older brothers are an inspiration to him as they follow their own interests, using the internet and books to find information. They are all frequent visitors to the local public library, and spend long periods out of doors with their parents or increasingly in a brotherhood, exploring the local area. The boys are now 15, 13, 11 and 5.

Their house has a large overgrown garden and a fence with a gate into fields and the wood beyond. From an early age, their parents have encouraged them by example to use the garden and local fields for exploration and adventures. The garden has a tree-house, dens, camps and a large and rambling climbing frame between two trees, with ropes, tyres and ladders suspended from various points. The boys get involved during the holidays in building and rebuilding these structures which are used for games of imagination, role-play and adventure, for picnics and for watching, catching and releasing creatures of all sorts.

A creative set of genes, a larger than average family and a large part of childhood spent out-of-doors and in the company of older brothers has shaped Oliver's brain, building on his natural interests for problem solving and creative thinking. He is now a real experimenter, with a brain that is constantly searching for new challenges and creative opportunities.

Key elements of the brain

Oliver is evidently a product of his nature or genes (his parents' education, careers and strong interest in creating and collecting information); his nurture (the way his parents have approached child-rearing) and his life chances (an environment that meets his needs, and plenty of models from his brothers of children who can create their own enjoyment and maintain a strong family bond).

We now know that being out-of-doors in childhood shapes children's brains in subtle and important ways, not least in ensuring a strong immune system. Outdoor experience in childhood fosters creativity and a brain in tune with nature. However, children seem to be even further away from nature than most of us were at their age. There is an inexorable slide towards the indoors, and children seem not only to be inexperienced in the natural world, but even frightened by its possible dangers.

'Within the space of a few decades, the way children understand and experience nature has changed radically. Today kids are aware of global threats to the environment, – but their physical contact, their intimacy with nature, is fading. Richard Louv, *Last Child in the Woods* (Algonquin Paperbacks 2008)

Oliver's outdoor experiences are crucial to his brain development and to the way he learns. The natural materials and the opportunities offered in the outdoor environment are almost without limit – from sticks and stones to water, sand, mud, frogs and rainbows. These 'loose parts' are always available, always new, and offer endless combinations, problems to solve and projects to explore.

'An example is found in Nicholson's theory of loose parts (1971). Nicholson proposes that there is a relationship between flexible environments and the level of creativity and inventiveness that they support. We can readily relate to the classic example of a 'loose parts environment', the seashore, with its shifting elements of water, sand, flotsam and jetsam.' Theresa Casey, 'Environments for Play' (www.playscotland.org September 2003)

Oliver is not only fortunate in his experience of the natural world and his freedom to explore it, but he is also one of the few children in his class with full attendance during his nursery and reception years. His outdoor life has worked with his place in a big family, to ensure a strong immune system, resistant to common bugs.

DP Strachan, in the British Medical Journal titled 'Hay fever, hygiene, and household size', 1989, found that children raised in environments with older children were exposed to more diseases at an earlier age and were healthier.

The development of language for communication and thinking is not only a central part of any early years programme, but an essential for learning throughout life. Oliver's brain development has been affected by the example of his older brothers, who have been encouraged to include him from his earliest days. He has always been in their company, they have always shown him love and have respected his opinion and point of view, and this has nurtured a faster development of language than might have been the case in a different family. Oliver now has a wide vocabulary, a good sense of imaginative language and unlike many five-year-olds he rarely makes mistakes in spoken tenses, verb forms or sentence construction such as 'runned' or 'builded'.

He is also very interested in writing for genuine purposes such as making his notice, which shows his emerging ability to hear, match and record sounds. He refers readily to books and other sources of information, and takes these into his imaginative thinking, confident that the key people in his life will respond warmly to all his efforts. This confidence makes him able to take risks in his thinking, his relationships and the activities he takes interest in. His sense of attachment is secure and this will affect his ability to learn and to retain learning in the short and long-term memory centres of his brain. How different Oliver's chances in life have been from those available to Michael!

Oliver's position on the gender spectrum must place him somewhere in the broad central range. His early and easy language response indicates a position towards the feminine end, his active body indicates the masculine end. This shows that gender placement is a complex discussion and we would do well to use such discussions as indicators rather than embedded certainties. However, it may be good to think about extreme feminine or masculine characteristics as we look at children whose behaviour is less extreme or less clear. Poets and musicians may well reside in the central part of the gender spectrum, as might female scientists or male teachers in the early years. The ideal mixture surely is one of characteristics from both gender stereotypes – kindness, consideration, strength of purpose, a sure grasp of language, strong relationships, creative thinking, the ability to concentrate on one thing when necessary; combined with the ability to multitask, loyalty to the group, and good interpersonal skills.

There is now emerging evidence that many men have brains structured to work more like those of women, and many women have brains structured to work like those of men. This is covered in more detail in Stevie's story (see page 111), where the concept of the 'bridge brain' is explored.

Oliver's place, well away from the extremes of either end, gives him a unique blend of capabilities and emphasises the individual nature of each child. Exploring Oliver's brain might reveal the following mixture:

- When Oliver thinks and talks he may well be using more of the language centres in his brain than many boys do. Other boys may be using just the right half of their brains for language, Oliver is certainly crossing through the corpus callosum to the left side of his brain in language activities.

- His behaviour is wide ranging – moving between action and reflection, as observed by adults when he suddenly becomes still in the midst of movement. He is able to manage and control activity, pausing when he wants to think. Oliver is spending plenty of time in his cortex, the thinking part of his brain, and seems to have early control of impulses, which might give him less control over his own behaviour.

- Oliver often starts thinking in the right hemisphere of his brain. This is where imagination and creativity are processed, but he is able to make good links to language development centres in his left brain, when he needs to discuss what he is thinking and planning.

- A male brain and the effects of testosterone affect the way he learns, making him persistent and tenacious once his interest is aroused. The story in this book describes how focused he can be.

- Feelings of fairness are features of strong groups of people, and Oliver's strong brotherhood at home has helped him to develop feelings of responsibility to the dragons, for taking their treasure, and a wish to make amends. Unlike many boys, oxytocin, the 'bonding' chemical is obviously present in Oliver's body and brain, making him more aware of others and able to display empathy.

- Oliver is interested in other children and always keen to involve them in his projects, but he is less tolerant of the single-minded action of the pack than many more boyish boys, and as they lose interest in him, he is quite prepared to continue his investigations with the quieter, more reflective children, often including girls.

- Models of his brothers' behaviour are very important and influential and these include conscientious fulfilling of intentions, consideration for others, a sense of responsibility unusual in a child of this age, and a mature willingness to let go of a project and move on to the next one, after acquiring what might be called 'a sense of closure'!

The Cleverness of Boys

Other influences

Of course, influences of nurture are very important to children's development, and so are parental attitudes to upbringing. Oliver's parents have a less usual style of upbringing. In encouraging the boys to look after each other and take responsibility for their group, they are not neglecting their children, but intending to strengthen character, social responsibility and independence. Oliver's mother's parents were very strict and his father was brought up by a lone mother, widowed at an early age and extremely protective. Both were single children, who longed for siblings and vowed to have large families. It is fortunate that they met!

These parents feel strongly that children should be encouraged to behave like a family and that the wide age range would enable this to happen with mother and father as equal and equally respected members of the group. It is unusual to see a group of children operating as this brotherhood does, and it is a credit to their parents that their support has enabled it to happen; not an abdication, but a genuine fostering of trust.

Another feature of Oliver's upbringing is that 'screen time' is strictly controlled, not an ever-present background to living. There is a television in the living room, but none of the boys has a TV in their bedroom, and when the television is on, the family tend to watch programmes or DVDs together. The computer is in the hall, next to the living room, where its use can also be monitored. Oliver's parents have read the research about early screen time, and want their boys to develop wide interests and not suffer the damage that excessive screen time can bring.

'Research continues to link excessive preschool screen time with language delay, obesity, attentional problems and even aggression depending upon content. At the same time, studies show that high quality preschool can be beneficial to children's development. Unfortunately, for many children, the potential benefits of preschool may be being displaced by passive TV viewing. I suspect many parents are unaware of the frequency and extent of TV viewing in day care settings. Hopefully, these findings will serve as a wake up call for them.' Dimitri A Christakis, 'Preschool-Aged Children's Television Viewing in Child Care Settings' in *Pediatrics* (December 2009)

These factors of their lives are not seen as a problem to the boys. Their interests are wide and they have busy lives, where TV is a part, but not a central part.

How to recognise and value the strengths of boys like Oliver

Oliver is an unusual boy and in some ways his brain is peculiar. His reflective nature and his upbringing have definitely had an effect on the strengths of his learning style and his personality, combining with his genetic make-up and the chance of his family background and nurture. His parents want him to continue to do well as he moves into his primary years, and maintain his interest and focus. However, they do realise that as the youngest child in a big family, he may have been over-protected by his brothers and perhaps indulged by everyone in the family. They know he will not be able to follow his single-minded projects for such long periods as he gets older, and that he will be expected to use his early language and thinking skills to address reading and writing tasks that are perhaps not of his own choosing.

When his parents come to parents' evenings, they are keen to discuss his future with staff, to make sure that his rather unusual early experiences are a benefit to him, not a handicap. They also realise that as the boys grow older, they may grow apart and eventually Oliver will be the only one at home, perhaps for most of his secondary schooling. They don't want him to be lonely, so they understand the need for him to make secure friendships outside the family. Here are some of the strategies that could help Oliver and boys like him as he moves on into primary school:

- Oliver doesn't have many close friends and his parents are aware that he could become isolated as he gets older.
  - The school will work with the parents to widen friendships and friendship groups, perhaps through a 'buddying' system with older children, joining some after-school activities or sports where older and younger children work and play together.
  - Innovative approaches, such as 'buddying' or spending work time with older children need to be used carefully, or they could just reinforce isolation.

- Language is important to Oliver, and his development has been faster than in many boys of his age. The language of home and the language of school may be very different. His brothers make no allowance for Oliver's age, and talk to and with him as if he were much older, often using complex technical vocabulary and sentence structure. In school, his peer group, aged from three to six, has a much more limited language code, with some children still using single words. Adults work hard to extend Oliver's

The Cleverness of Boys

language, but this is a challenge for them, as their priorities and externally set targets are often to raise the levels of the most needy, not the most able language users.

- The teachers in the primary classes should now look at ways of working flexibly across year groups, so children like Oliver have the chance to meet and work with more mature language users in mixed age and mixed ability groups.

- Oliver needs to be challenged.
  - His teachers have begun to construct increasingly complex provocations and longer projects to interest him. He is encouraged to work on these at home and at school, involving both his family and his growing circle of school friends. These projects are not just linked to his existing interests in nature, music, and construction. They will involve him in reading, writing, discussing and researching in other areas of learning, following interests in history, geography and maths, and in writing and reading stories.

- Oliver needs plenty of time to think, research and use knowledge in different ways, but he also needs to work with other children of his own age.
  - The school fosters group work where children can use their individual skills while contributing to a more structured group. These groups will use creative thinking tools such as mind maps, diagrams and other ways of recording ideas and findings, displaying these during projects so that everyone can follow the progress of the work.

- ICT may be a key to learning for Oliver, and the use of a wide range of ICT across the school is already established.
  - Encourage Oliver to access these resources (including metal detectors, DVD and digital cameras, digital microscopes) as well as continuing to use the Internet and books, to expand his research. These will also be used to record creative thinking and offer real reasons for writing.

- Oliver is very good at focusing on one thing, and gets more involved in activities than many other children:
  - Provide an early warning of the end of an activity periods to help Oliver to change tack and concentrate on the next activity. Transition time, when he can 'wind down' one activity before embarking on another, is very helpful to imaginative and creative minds. It gives space to return from another world, another character, another story, and to bring their

activities to a comfortable end. This will reduce stress and frustration, which interferes with learning.

- Give him plenty of time for activities he is interested in. Oliver is used to long uninterrupted periods of play at home, so try to make child-initiated activity time as long as possible, and offer this early in the day, so he has time to follow his interests *before* you ask him to sit and listen to you and other children.
- Large motor activity just before a spell of fine motor activity is particularly helpful for energetic boys, so if you are going to embark on a concentrated activity, make sure he has had some physical activity just before you start. Try vigorous action songs, a simple brain break activity or perhaps paired activities such as throwing and catching, to encourage engagement with others.

Oliver's parents, his teachers and his brothers will need to watch carefully as he grows into the next stage of his life. The work on broadening his interests and friendship groups must not be at the expense of his relationship with his family. The 'brotherhood' will be important to him for the rest of his life, so his parents are determined to support the continuing relationship between their sons. They are planning holidays and other activities to reinforce the bond, so the enduring friendship has as much chance as possible of surviving the rigours of adolescence and early adulthood.

His teachers need to be aware that unusually creative children like Oliver are sometimes missed when identifying gifted and talented members of a group. Significant characteristics of giftedness include keen powers of observation and a sense of the significant, an eye for important details, a questioning attitude and seeking information for its own sake as much as for its usefulness. Gifted children often have a large storehouse of information about a variety of topics, which they can recall quickly, and can often make valid generalisations about events, people, or objects. They quickly perceive similarities, differences, and anomalies. They are fluent and flexible thinkers, good guessers, and show emotional responsibility. Oliver has many of these talents, and sensitive guidance as he moves through the education system will be crucial in achieving success and fulfilment.

(Gifted children)'... may appear to do fine on their own. But without proper challenge they can become bored and unruly. As the years go by they may find it harder and harder as work does become more challenging, since they never faced challenge before'. The Rhode Island State Advisory Committee on Gifted and Talented Education (www.ri.net/gifted_talented/rhode.html)

Shawn the friend

Shawn's story

The pirate ship was finished and the big moment had arrived. It was time for Shawn to contact Rosco the pirate and tell him that his new ship was ready for inspection. But perhaps I should explain!

Rosco is a pirate puppet that a talented colleague and I used as part of a creative exchange with her reception class. In response to the children's interest in beaches and the sea, we had begun by introducing a strange-looking female puppet. Appearing rather prehistoric and sporting a shaggy dress and with a bone in her hair, I told the children that I had found her on a beach. The girls took to her immediately. They named her Bella and then they fed her, read to her, took her to the writing corner and speculated endlessly on where she had come from and what she might like to do. Not so the boys! I'm afraid that our prehistoric female friend held little interest for them.

Then, enter Rosco the pirate puppet, and they were hooked! They researched in books and on the Internet to find out all they could about pirates, and they really enjoyed having him around until one day an important letter arrived and he was summoned back to his ship. The letter read as follows:

The High Seas
11th December 2009

Dear Rosco,

We have heard that you have been visiting some children in a school in Birmingham. We hope that you have had a nice time. However, we are writing to you now as we need you back on the ship urgently! We have been in a bad storm and the ship is badly damaged and needs lots of repairs. We need all hands on deck if we are to get the ship ready for sailing to Paradise Island in time for Christmas. Please return to us as fast as you can as no other pirate can mend sails as well as you!

Hoping to see you soon,

Captain Sharkfin and the crew.

Obviously, the boys were extremely disappointed to find that Rosco was leaving them, and none more than Shawn. He had really enjoyed all of the work around Rosco, but we were not altogether prepared for what followed. Shawn was one of those wiry, athletic five-year-olds who never seemed to be still for more than 30 seconds at a time, so it was unusual to see him sitting in the book corner lost in thought. However, this period of inactivity was short lived and before long he was flying around the classroom like a whirlwind with a trail of other boys behind him.

By snack time they had re-organised the tables in the creative area and gathered together a range of resources that comprised a large cardboard box, paper, fabric, tape, scissors and glue. Before long, Rosco's new ship was under construction. Shawn made it clear that he felt very sorry for Rosco and that it was important that he did whatever he could to help him. What really struck us though, was the time and commitment that went into this emotionally-charged project. Over three days, the box was transformed into a magnificent ship complete with mast, sails, steering wheel, compass and a resident parrot, and the big moment arrived for Rosco to be introduced to his new craft.

As part of the project we had equipped Rosco with a 'pay as you go' mobile phone so that the children could communicate with him via text messages, so Rosco was duly sent a text, and sure enough, he returned the next day to inspect the new ship. Shawn had even gone to the trouble of making him a new hat and a telescope, with which, as I am sure you can imagine, Rosco was entranced!

Having Bella and Rosco in the classroom had also prompted the children to explore the relationship between them, and when they disappeared together the children speculated on where they had gone.

'I think they've got married and Bella's had a baby because when they make friends they get married. When you're nearly a teenager you make really best friends and when the girl gets pregnant you're wife and husband,' suggested Rosina.

'Or a big crocodile ate them or a shark. I think the crocodile ate Rosco and the shark ate Bella and a stingray stung Bella and Rosco and they were both crying,' said Remah.

'I think Rosco's thinking he'll take her shopping. Maybe he likes her. He'll buy ice cream and lettuce and salad and a leek and a yoghurt. They go for money because if they have no money they'll starve won't they?' explained Zahra.

'They might ask someone for some money,' said Remah.

'And then they'll have loads of food and they'll be happy. If they look at each other and smile at each other they'll be friends. I think they'll buy some toys. If they get married they'll have a baby.' said Zahra. It was interesting to note the way in which the girls, in the main, focused on the more domestic of possibilities while the boys were more adventurous in their ideas.

'Anyway,' said Shawn, 'Rosco's most probably gone to look for treasure, and if he has he won't take Bella with him!'

We enquired why not. 'Because you can't get lady pirates!' Shawn explained emphatically. Again I asked why not.

Shawn looked at me as if I was rather stupid! 'Because they don't like swords or guns or anything that's dangerous and they don't like getting sliced!' he continued.

'So if Rosco's gone to look for treasure, what might Bella be doing?' I asked.

Shawn looked thoughtful and then said, 'Bella might go to fairyland and play with fairies and some toys'.

Anxious to explore this further I said, 'So, if Bella's gone to fairyland to play with fairies and toys would Rosco go with her?'

'No, Rosco doesn't like those things! He just wants treasure and boy things,' said Shawn, looking at me as if I was quite out of my mind.

Following this conversation, we speculated on where to take the provocation from here, and decided that we would have Bella and Rosco return together with a chest full of treasure. By this time, various other members of staff, including the headteacher, had become involved in the story so it was agreed that he would tell the children that voices had been heard in the cupboard next to his office. When this exciting piece of news was shared with the children they were convinced that it must be Bella and Rosco. The cupboard was ceremoniously opened in their presence to reveal the two puppets, complete with a large treasure chest.

To say that the children were excited would be the understatement of the year. It was all we could do to stop them diving headlong into the cupboard. Shawn was at the front of the group, beside himself with elation. 'Look,' he said, as he opened the treasure chest to see what was inside, 'real money, and gold cups and jewels and stuff, there's loads in here!' The rest of the group began to gather treasure and, by a process of degrees it was returned to the classroom where there was much discussion about where Bella and Rosco could have found so much treasure.

'They might have brought it from Australia,' suggested Ellie.

'No,' said Isabel. 'They don't have money in Australia!'

'Yes they do,' insisted Ellie. 'My dad lives there.'

While the girls argued Remah had been thinking. 'Rosco said we are allowed to have a little bit of the treasure,' he announced.

'No we can't!' said Gus. 'It belongs to Rosco.'

'We might be able to ask Bella and Rosco if we can borrow some of the money,' suggested Zahra.

'And then we can share it with the other class,' added Rosina.

Remah looked doubtful. 'But there might not be enough!' he said.

As the argument about what should happen to the treasure continued I noticed that Shawn had become very quiet, and was just wondering why this should be, when he suddenly brought the discussion to an abrupt end by announcing loudly, 'We should give it to some people 'cos we don't need it. It would be greedy. We should give it to people who have no money. We could give it to the old people. Or we could give it to some people like in Africa, where they are poor and don't have any money'.

'Some people in Africa are rich,' protested Gus.

'No they're not,' said Shawn, 'they don't have nothing in Africa. No shoes or socks because they have sand and they don't have any taps and they have to get water from the lake and have a bath in the lake and they have to sleep on the ground or in a tent. African people need lots 'cos they have no money, and anyway, Rosco's changed his mind now. He wants to help the poor people in Africa 'cos he doesn't want to be mean any more.'

We watched amazed at Shawn's passion and powers of persuasion, for nobody thought to argue with him, although there was some dispute about exactly how the money should be spent. Some of the children wanted to buy clean water for an African community whereas some wanted to buy vegetables or a goat. In the end the matter was resolved by the use of voting circles. These were drawn in the outside area and the children were invited to make a mark in the circle that represented the way in which they thought the money should be spent. When the votes were counted there was overwhelming support for the clean water. So, the treasure was sold, and the money donated to a charity that would provide clean water for a village in Africa.

Shawn was triumphant and later that day as I watched him hurtling round the garden it occurred to me that I should not have been surprised at what he had accomplished. Because he was such a macho little boy, full of stories of pirates, weapons and fights, it was easy to forget that he was also extremely sensitive to the needs of others. Was it not Shawn who had befriended a tearful John on his first day at a new school? I remembered also the way in which he had organised a charity collection for orphans in India and painted a picture for Zahra when her guinea pig had died. Yes indeed, it was all too easy to stereotype children, especially boys! I made a mental note to try harder in future!

The Cleverness of Boys

How Shawn's brain affects his behaviour

Shawn's brain is also in overdrive, but in a different way from the other boys in the book. His ability to motivate a group, combined with his impetuous attack on the latest project makes him like Oliver, Donovan and Paul, but his leadership qualities, and his obsession with construction drive him in a different direction. He always has a practical project under way, making, fixing, doing, building, and, unlike Oliver, he is only happy in this work if other children are with him.

Making and taking things apart is a very common 'cleverness' of boys. Their interest in objects, and particularly in moving objects is present from birth and will drive them to throw, bang, hit and deconstruct any object they encounter. Research on baby boys and girl has revealed a great difference in behaviour, particularly with objects. Oestrogen and oxytocin in the bodies and brains of most girls (and some boys) encourage them to nurture dolls, soft toys and other children. This effect, which is triggered by contact and the shape of the human face, has been described as 'social glue'. Boys are more likely to be affected by testosterone and vasopressin, both of which result in action, experiment and sometimes aggression:

'Little boys when given dolls to play with, more often than girls pull the heads off, hit them against a table, throw them in the air, or generally engage in some kind of physical, kinesthetic, or spatial play with the dolls.' Michael Gurian, *The Minds of Boys* (Jossey Bass 2005)

Shawn shows this inclination as he explores the world, and he always has a project on hand, his enthusiasm inspiring others to join him. The creative drive almost always results in a concrete object – a den made from boxes or branches, a complex construction of blocks, a model made from recycled materials, or a small-world environment for superheroes or dinosaurs. The well developed right hemisphere of his brain works on 'big picture' solutions in three dimensions and big shapes, and his active learning style supports big movements and whole body involvement, preferably with a group of others to help him.

However, Shawn's left brain hemisphere is now getting in on the act! As he works on models and structures, he needs fine motor skills to fix, cut, join, stick and balance the pieces of his constructions. He is learning through practice how to use tools and equipment, and this is encouraging links between left and right hemispheres through the corpus callosum, the superhighway between the left and right brain, linking big picture with detail.

He is becoming ever more dextrous as he works, persevering when things get difficult and constantly thinking about how he can improve what he is doing. This repeated practice and repetition is strengthening the links between brain cells, coating them with a fatty substance called myelin, which protects and speeds up the messages. Practice of skills, particularly when Shawn is well motivated and using physical movement and language as he works, will increasingly 'hard wire' learning, making it permanent. This will last throughout his life, as the skills and abilities will come easily to him, and he will use them with enjoyment. 'Soft wired', learning which is not practised and revisited, or has been taught rather than learned through action, is easy prey to stress and often falls away, just as late revision for a driving test or exam may fall away once the test is over, or worse, as soon as the examiner starts to speak!

Shawn's creative mind and increasingly coordinated body are supported by good language development and a sociable nature, which enable him to organise groups and influence decisions in a stimulating early years environment.

'Since we don't know yet – if we ever will – how to speed up physiological readiness, the best advice is to concentrate on what we do know how to do: provide an array of interesting, curiosity stimulating objects and experiences, be available to provide a 'scaffold' to challenge new learning, and let the growing brain take what it needs.' Jane M Healy, *Your Child's Growing Mind* (Broadway 2004)

Key elements of the brain

Shawn has inherited his wiry, agile body and his 'masculine' brain almost entirely from his father, who is proudly Irish in both behaviour and loyalty. He is the foreman for a team of builders, who pride themselves on efficient work within their gang, strong leadership and loyalty. Shawn's brain will have been strongly affected by the masculine genes from his father. He will not only be more masculine by nature, but he will produce more testosterone in his body during his childhood. He will be naturally more active and even more aggressive than most girls, and more susceptible to the stresses of life. However, his father has a gentle side and this, combined with the nurture in his family enables him to respond in a more measured way than many of his peers. Shawn's nurture has been within a family where the leadership style of his father is paramount. 'You don't let people down, you pull your weight in the team, you inspire others, and you provide the "social glue" between team members.'

This family and work philosophy is tempered by Shawn's father's view of the place of women! He is a loving father and husband, remembers his wife's birthday and their wedding anniversary, and never shows any anger or violence in the home. But Shawn's mum doesn't work, and has not worked since she got married.

His father thinks that men should be the breadwinners, women should make the home and provide the comforts that the breadwinner has paid for. He thinks that children should be brought up in homes where mothers are there after school and in the holidays, and Shawn's mother is content to do just that. This less common family structure has had a great effect, not only on Shawn, but on his two older sisters. They are extremely feminine and spend most of their time playing with 'girls' toys' and proudly wear t-shirts with 'Daddy's Princess' on the front.

Aspirations for Shawn are in some ways higher than for his sisters. His father's benign dominance over the family reinforces a view that boys are more significant than girls, and that advantages of education should favour boys. This might seem an old-fashioned view, but research indicates that girls are more likely to achieve their aspirations than boys, so maybe Shawn does need an extra push from his dad!

'There are a number of key players in supporting aspirations, particularly parents, whose early influence can be crucial. Those working with parents, especially in disadvantaged areas, need to be aware that they can play a role in helping them develop these early aspirations and attitudes not only for their children, but for themselves. This will give them a sense of confidence and empowerment that they can help their children and persevere to overcome obstacles when things are not going well.' Leslie Morrison Gutman and Rodie Akerman, *Determinants of Aspirations* (Centre for Research on the Wider Benefits of Learning Institute of Education June 2008)

Nurture *does* have an effect on children and their learning, but whether this nurture is the result of chance, genetics, present culture or something else is food for constant debate. Shawn's view was that '... you can't get lady pirates! Because they don't like swords or guns of anything that's dangerous and they don't like getting sliced!' and that Bella might '... go to fairyland and play with fairies and some toys'. Does this reflect his father's view, his sisters' influence, or the pressure that our 21st century culture imposes on children? A culture where there are different toys for girls and boys, different clothes, different colours, and an assumption that all girls are princesses and all boys are superheroes.

Although he is obviously a very active, masculine boy, Shawn's place on the gender spectrum may have moved towards the masculine end as a result of his nurture, encouraged to show behaviours that are active and dominating, physical and noisy. However, his early language development and his sociability that balances persuasion with providing a strong and sensitive role model for others, indicate that he has some characteristics we would describe as more 'feminine'. As with many of the boys in this book, gender and sexual influence are complicated by culture and the chance of individual upbringing, including the chance influence of his neighbours, which we explore below.

'Both popular and scientific explanations of behavior, accustomed to invoking genes, parents, and society, seldom acknowledge the enormous role that unpredictable factors must play in the development of an individual.' Steven Pinker, *The Blank Slate* (Penguin 2003)

So how does the combination of nature, nurture, culture and chance affect Shawn's development and influence his learning and behaviour?

- Shawn's nature, nurture and culture drive his brain to explore, invent and construct. This is a natural feature of the brains of most children, but is particularly noticeable in boys. The nature of exploration in most boys is through touching, manipulating and sometimes destruction. Every time Shawn has an idea or is inspired to solve a problem, a picture seems to appear in his mind, a practical solution through action. Boys are better than most girls at manipulating 3D objects in their brains, and this makes them turn instinctively to construction.

- Commitment and loyalty are hallmarks of this family, his father is a working example of this within his team, and he brings his expectations home, where they become standards for his children. Using actions and feelings together involves both sides of the brain, and for Shawn this means reasoning in language as he thinks about others. These character traits will emerge in many situations, such as in resolving the dilemma about what to do with the pirate treasure.

- Shawn is a secure, well attached boy, and this will support his brain growth. Less attached boys are constantly struggling with the stress chemicals which flood the brain when they feel anxious, and stress chemicals erode the developing links between brain cells. Shawn has had a close relationship with his mother, the support of his immediate and extended family, and this will help him at school and throughout life. Like Leroy, with strong attachment, he has high self-esteem, good relationships with others, a clearly developed conscience and a sense of fairness, curiosity and confidence. These are all characteristics of children with secure attachment. Making friends and relating to others are easy for Shawn, and he is constantly attended by a group of other children, mostly boys.

The Cleverness of Boys

- The leadership skills that Shawn demonstrates have their roots in security, the leadership style of his father, and encouragement from his mother and significant members of his community. They also involve him increasingly in using both sides of his brain, the right side for action, and feelings, the left side for language and planning.

- His mother, although quiet and apparently dominated by his father, is actually a strong character, and a significant influence in the development of all her children. She encourages them to make decisions and take the lead, even in simple activities such as sorting the washing, planning menus, making shopping lists and preparing for outings. She spent time with them before they went to school, not only telling stories, visiting the park and making cakes, but challenging their thinking by asking 'What if...?' and 'I wonder why...?'. She also made sure that their horizons were not limited by life with a 'stay at home' mum, getting involved in many activities in the community, including having a successful allotment. She is always present when they watch television after school and in the early evening, helping them to make choices, discuss events, and particularly to talk about the early evening news bulletin, which is rarely missed. And she is still on hand to help with homework, discuss the day and offer ideas for following up their interests. This constant feature of Shawn's early life has supported strong brain development and enquiry skills.

- Shawn's mum has also been influential in his early language development and sense of creativity, encouraging links between the right and left hemispheres, as the right side processes music and the left side organises the words. Music, songs, nursery rhymes and stories played a significant part in the children's young lives, and they still do. Shawn's mum has a great sense of fun, and she would always be prepared to get involved in their suggestions of making a den under the bedclothes, having a kitchen band with saucepans and wooden spoons, or drawing monsters on the back path with the chalky stones they dug up in the garden.

  Shawn's mum didn't know it, but experiencing a sense of fun, an ability to use rhythm and beat, and creative use of familiar objects all give children a significant edge in early school activities and a long-term boost to reading, writing and creative thinking.

- The language of persuasion is a subtle language, and most children don't acquire it until later in their development. However, despite the findings that boys generally have more difficulty processing feelings in words, and their single focus tendency can make them inflexible, no difference was made in the treatment of Shawn and his sisters. Shawn has nearly six years' experience of negotiating and listening to others doing the same. His brain will be challenged to respond by exploring feelings and expressing these in words.

During these activities, Shawn's brain will be functioning more like a female brain, using language sites in both sides of his brain, and probably producing the bonding chemicals of oxytocin and oestrogen. The children take part in discussions about where to go on holiday or for outings at the weekend. What to watch on television is fairly decided, as there is only one set in the house. Decisions on meals have been made collaboratively ever since the children were old enough to express preferences.

Other influences

As mentioned earlier, Shawn is not only the product of nature, nurture and culture, he is also, like all of us, the result of chance:

'... the unexplained variance in personality throws a spotlight on the role of sheer chance in development: random differences in prenatal blood supply and exposure to toxins, pathogens, hormones, and antibodies; random differences in the growth or adhesion of axons in the developing brain; random events in experience; random differences in how a stochastically (randomly) functioning brain reacts to the same events in experience.' Steven Pinker, 'Why Nature and Nurture Won't go Away' (*Daedalus* Magazine 2004)

One significant chance that may have affected Shawn's behaviour in the story we quote is that he chanced to live next to Marilyn and Paul. The close relationship that developed between the two families began with smiles and conversations over the back fence as Shawn's mum hung out the washing, or tended her herb garden when Shawn was a baby. Cups of tea and chats in each other's kitchens followed, and as confidence and friendship grew Marilyn's offer to baby-sit was gratefully received by Shawn's busy parents.

As the years passed and the two women became good friends, Marilyn and Paul became a part of Shawn's extended family. The very special influence that they had on Shawn was when he went to visit them, squeezing through the gap in the hedge to enter a house that was more like a museum. On every surface of every room were interesting objects – a huge fir cone, a cog from the engine of a lorry, a postcard from a strange land, a storybook from Paul's childhood. In one corner of the living room is the most fantastic dressing-up box, in another is a box of 'small parts' – buttons, reels, boxes, ribbon, string, buckles, beads, washers and so on. New objects are added, but none is ever removed, because each has a story to tell.

Paul and Marilyn have no children of their own, so the kids next door have become their substitute, benefiting from their amazing collection of objects and stories. Paul is an engineer, Marilyn works part time in an Oxfam charity shop, and both have had an influence on Shawn and his sisters. Paul's childhood in Africa and Marilyn's in the Welsh countryside provide a wealth of stories and real-life adventures. The atlas is a frequent reference book as they tell their stories, and Paul's shed, where models and constructions are hanging everywhere, is a magical place for experiment and testing.

It is a credit to Shawn's parents that they are prepared to share their children, realising what the advantages will be. Shawn's grandparents are all in Ireland, and he sees them infrequently. Paul and Marilyn provide a great enhancement to life and particularly to his creativity and imagination and his sense of responsibility and charity.

How to recognise and value the strengths of boys like Shawn

Family stability and high expectations, a secure and stimulating early childhood, and involvement of his parents in supporting his learning should ensure that Shawn does well in school, as long as both his 'clevernesses' *and* his needs are recognised. His parents, although confident in many ways, have always found it difficult to speak out at parents' meetings. Despite their shared convictions about they way they have brought up their children and their hopes for the future, they still remember their own school days in Ireland, in schools run by nuns or priests whose response to parents was at most civil, and at least dismissive and blaming. However, as their youngest child and only boy, Shawn is a precious child to both of them. His future success is very important to them, and they have made a good relationship with his reception teacher, where conversations can be open and informative to everyone. These are some of the things they have discussed and the strategies they have decided might help him:

- Shawn needs support for continuing creativity and creative thinking. They agree that Shawn's successful year in reception is due to the child-initiated learning opportunities and chances to take his interests further in construction and imagination. The early years curriculum states:

'Being creative involves the whole curriculum, not just the arts. It is not necessarily about making an end-product such as a picture, song or play. Children will more easily make connections between things they've learned if the environment encourages them to do so. For example, they need to be able to fetch materials easily and to be able to move them from one place to another.' *Practice Guidance for the Early Years Foundation Stage*, (DCSF 2008)

- The teachers in the primary classes are reconsidering the current curriculum structure and the division of this into subject areas. They are intending to follow suggestions in recent reports that successful learning happens when subjects are 'joined up' and topics and themes encourage creative thinking. This should result in '... a well-planned, vibrant curriculum (which) recognises that primary children relish learning independently and cooperatively; they love to be challenged and engaged in practical activities; they delight in the wealth of opportunities for understanding more about the world; and they readily empathise with others through working together and through experiences in the arts, literature, religious education and much else.' *Independent Review of the Primary Curriculum*, (DCSF 2009)

- Another challenge for Shawn's parents and teachers is to help him manage his strong sense of leadership, which could make him a dominant character in any class, and eventually this might be a position he won't want to give up to anyone else.
  - His father knows the importance of leadership, but also the need for good team members. Shawn needs to be able to be both, and his father's model may make him reluctant to be just a team member! His father decided to join an amateur football club where he would never be good enough to be the captain, so he could model being a reliable team member. This was not easy for a natural leader, but he worked at it and really enjoyed the support Shawn and his sisters gave at every match, after which they all went for pizza and talked about football together.

- Focus is an issue for most boys. They are able to focus on something that interests them for considerable periods but *changing focus* is often really difficult for them. Shawn's parents and teachers, who become very frustrated by this feature of his behaviour have talked about some strategies:
  - Early warnings may help. Tell Shawn five minutes before bedtime or a change of activity to give him the time he needs to wind up one thought or action and be ready for the next.

- Give him a body and brain break (something with movement, beat or songs) to help with the transition between activities. Even when boys are working on activities that they have initiated themselves, they get really absorbed and need a chance to fidget and move around. This break is particularly important if you want them to do something that involves sitting down and listening to you!
- Boys' brains enter a 'rest state' many more times per day than girls. This is the state when boys gaze, switch off, or even seem to doze; 'A boy's brain 'shuts off' more times a day than a girl's brain tends to do – as a result boys and girls have different approaches to paying attention, visioning their future, completing a task, de-stressing, feeling emotions, relating to others, becoming bored, and even having basic conversations.' Michael Gurian, *The Purpose of Boys* (Jossey-Bass 2009)

  Shawn is one of these boys. Recognise this feature and understand when boys are in a rest state and when they are deliberately not listening. Saying a child's name before you ask them to do something or listen to you will help. All the adults now use children's names before they speak, to ensure they are listening. This avoids frustration for everyone.
- Girls hear better throughout life than boys, who find long sentences and complex instructions difficult. Teachers and parents would do well to realise that some six-year-old boys find it difficult to understand sentences or instructions of more than eight words. Boys often find eye contact harder to maintain than girls, so teachers and parents at Shawn's school are encouraged to make eye contact, but keep instructions short and simple. Some children find it easier to remember instructions if they repeat them several times out loud (or in their heads) as they prepare for the activity or move towards a different part of the room.

- Shawn has good powers of reasoning and skills of persuasion and is usually able to talk others into agreeing with him. He is also very keen to ensure fairness and justice, and these qualities are to be admired and fostered. However, Shawn will need to learn how to lose an argument, concede a loss or relinquish leadership. The stories and reminiscences shared by Paul and Marilyn, and the models of his parents were the roots of Shawn's sense of community and charity.
  - Underpin these experiences at school with a strong programme of citizenship, including the use of Philosophy for Children, Persona Doll work, the SEAL programme and getting involved in school and local charity work. In these activities, Shawn will be able to explore alternative views, lifestyles and philosophical positions.

- Shawn's family are just beginning to feel relaxed in school. They need to know that the teachers welcome their contribution, admire the way they have brought up their children, and are willing to help to ensure that Shawn and his sisters do well.

Shawn comes to school with the support of a strong and extended family, and as described in a recent Government White Paper:

'Effective parenting plays a critical role in shaping children's wellbeing, achievements and prospects from the early years onwards. Emotional bonds are crucial for neurological development and positive early years experiences have long-term effects on development. Nurturing relationships and secure attachments between mothers and fathers and their children contribute towards a broad range of later capabilities, such as love of learning, social skills and self-esteem. Supporting parenting is therefore a crucial part of ensuring that family provides the best possible environment within which individuals can develop.' *Supporting parental involvement to strengthen early years attachments and encourage learning* (HM Government 2009)

We can only hope that with this sort of support, things will continue to go well with Shawn as he moves out of pirates and into primary school!

Stevie the actor

Stevie's story

As I stared at Stevie's picture in my photograph album the memories came flooding back! In an instant, I was standing outside the home corner listening to Yasmine's squeals of protest as Stevie banished her from the proceedings.

'You can't play in here,' he affirmed, 'because me and Louise and Samantha's putting on a puppet show and it ain't ready for the audience yet. Anyway, you have to buy a ticket and we ain't made 'em yet!'

'Well I want to be in the puppet show then,' said Yasmine, trying to stand up to him, but I could see she was wasting her time! Stevie leaned forward with his hands on his hips.

'Well you can't be!' he replied emphatically, 'Only me and Louise and Samantha is doing this show, there ain't no-one else allowed.' Yasmine poked her tongue out as a way of registering her dissatisfaction with the situation, but realizing she was beaten, retreated to the book corner.

I watched from a distance as the three friends rearranged the furniture in preparation for the show, and it didn't take me long to realize what they were doing. Working with puppets was a regular feature of our early years unit, and as I watched I quickly became aware of what was happening.

'Now', said Stevie, who was clearly in charge, 'I'm going to be Mrs Bayley. Samantha, you've got to be Mrs Broadbent, and Louise can be Mrs Pritchard and do the signing for the deaf kids!' I know it is not unusual for young children to copy the behaviour and actions of the people they spend their time with, but here, as I continued to watch with interest, I realized that we were being skilfully and accurately mimicked.

The two large puppets we used for our story sessions were kept in a large drawstring bag which resided in a discreet hiding place in the stock room when not in use. Stevie had selected a large shopping bag from the dressing-up area and found two anatomically correct dolls to represent Wally and Betsy our puppets. He placed them in the bag and sat down on a chair. Placing the bag on his lap, and copying all my mannerisms with horrifying accuracy he said, 'Now, I want all you children to look this way and listen, and when you are ready, Wally and Betsy will come out of the bag'. Then, with a theatrical shake of his head, he drew the dolls from the bag and sat them on his knee, just as he had observed me do with the puppets.

'Now, Samantha, which story are you gunna tell?' and before Samantha could answer, 'Do the one when Wally and Betsy flooded the toilets, that's a good one that is!'

'OK then,' said Samantha compliantly, and as she began the story I could see that she also had a great gift for mimicry! As the story proceeded, Louise waved her arms around attempting a not too convincing approximation of British Sign Language.

'Louise,' shouted Stevie, obviously not impressed. Do it properly, like what Mrs Pritchard does!' It was fortuitous that at this moment the bell rang for tidy-up time, for I fear that Louise was never going to meet Stevie's high expectations.

'Oh no,' he wailed disappointedly, 'we ain't got no more time now, we'll just have to finish the show off tomorrow'. I smiled to myself as I addressed myself to the task of helping with the tidying up. What I had just witnessed was so typically Stevie!

Each morning and afternoon there was a short session when all the children and staff met as a large group for stories and songs, and these sessions were one of Stevie's favourite times of the day. He listened to the stories with rapt attention and was the first to leap to his feet when we needed an actor. He loved nothing more than to play a part in the acting out of a fairy tale, and the bigger the part the more he enjoyed it. I remembered him in the role of Rapunzel. He stood on a stage block, his jumper on his head to represent her long hair, and solemnly let down his hair for the witch. (At his request this role was played by Samantha!)

It seemed that Stevie, Samantha and Louise were quite inseparable. He was completely besotted with them, to the extent that he continued with the habit of wearing his cardigan on his head so that, as he put it, he could have long hair just like Samantha and Louise!

Then there was the day we did *The Three Billy Goats Gruff*. At the first indication that this was to be acted out Stevie was on his feet yelling, 'I've got to be the troll. Please let me be the troll. I'll die if I can't be the troll'. Then, with characteristic melodrama, he threw himself on his knees with his hands clasped together as if in prayer.

'Well let's see Stevie,' I said, trying to be fair, 'we'd better just check whether there's anyone else who would like to be the troll.' Fortunately there wasn't, so with visible relief, Stevie threw himself into position under the bridge in readiness for his appearance as the troll. Then, once the Billy Goats Gruff were cast, we were ready to begin.

It was my custom to tell the story, pausing at intervals to allow the children to tell the bits that they could do for themselves, but I don't think that anyone was quite prepared for Stevie's memorable lines in his role as the troll. Perhaps it was just the way he had heard it, but most of the staff had to work hard to stifle their amusement when he leapt up from beneath the bridge, pointed at the Little Billy Goat Gruff and asked loudly and clearly, 'Who's that crip crapping across my bridge?' Captivated by the power of his performance this pearl was lost on the children and I resolved to spend some time with him practising the 'tr' sound!

Stevie was also very popular with out local vicar who visited the early years unit once a week to tell stories. These were frequently bible stories, which, much to Stevie's approval, the vicar liked the children to 'act out' as he told them. I well remember the telling of the Easter Story. Generally, Stevie was one of the first to be assigned a role, but perhaps on this particular occasion the vicar thought someone else should get a look in! I watched as the parts were being cast and I saw Stevie's lip quiver as he faced the possibility of not getting one. Then as the players took their positions and the vicar began the story Stevie put up his hand and shouted loudly in desperation, 'Well, if all the other parts are gone, please can I be the pieces of silver?' Such was his passion for acting that even such a minor role was better than none!

Indeed, Stevie revelled in any opportunity to be dramatic, spending hours in the imaginative play area, usually with Samantha and Louise but artfully engaging the services of additional children when a larger cast was required. For most of the time Stevie played with the girls. He really enjoyed their company, and while I think some of the boys found this strange, he was so popular that none of them ever passed comment. In fact, when he took to dressing up in a ballet tutu on a daily basis nobody seemed to mind, for dancing was another of his passions.

Even at four years old he could do wonderful things with a few lengths of net curtain. He would wrap himself up then dance elf-like around the unit, usually wearing the famous jumper around his head. He also knew the words to all the latest songs and was invaluable at times when performance art was needed for assemblies, end-of-term concerts or, in later years, for school plays.

As Stevie progressed through the school it became apparent that he was probably not going to be academic, but his talent for acting went from strength to strength. At the age of nine he gave an incredible performance as the Artful Dodger in a production of Oliver. Although he had struggled with reading and writing, he learned the words for the part at the speed of light and picked up the songs with accuracy and precision, to say nothing of his excellent interpretation. When it was time for rehearsals he was always the first there, and he never missed a single one. His concentration was immense and when anyone forgot their words he spoke them for them. It was as if he knew the entire script by heart.

As the production drew nearer he spoke of nothing else, spending hours drawing pictures of the various characters in the musical. He designed his own costume and had strong ideas about how everyone else should be dressed, and when the time for the performances finally arrived he was ecstatic with anticipation. He also sold ticket after ticket to friends, family and neighbours, and, if you haven't guessed already, he stole the show! I don't think I have ever seen anyone quite so happy.

Stevie loved every minute of being part of the musical and was desperately sad when it came to an end and the set was dismantled. I remember telling him not to worry because we would soon be starting on the Christmas production of Aladdin. In this production he gave an equally powerful performance in the role of Widow Twanky, enjoying it every bit as much as his role as the Artful Dodger. Stevie seemed to be such a natural actor that many of us wondered if this was something that he could maybe do professionally.

When Stevie left us to move on to secondary education he was sadly missed, not only for his acting ability but also because of the unique power of his personality. Stevie was interested in everyone. An interested listener and a lively conversationalist, he would sustain long conversations with everyone from the lunchtime supervisors, the site manger and cleaners to visiting lecturers and Ofsted inspectors. There were few people he would not approach and most would feel the richer for time spent in his company.

I remember meeting Stevie shortly after he had left school. Having not seen him for a long time I enquired what he was doing, and wondered if it would involve any acting. He told me proudly that he was working in a care home for the elderly. He was obviously really enjoying it and I could just imagine the old people's delight as he entertained them with stories, songs and conversation!

How Stevie's brain affects his behaviour

Stevie's story takes us further in his school experience than the other boys in this book, and this will enable us to look back on his early education in some detail, identifying what worked and what didn't, and how his behaviour and reactions changed over the years. We can follow his development into

The Cleverness of Boys

secondary school and the challenges boys like him face as they grow into adolescence.

The brains of boys like Stevie are even more complex than the brains we have examined so far in this book. Because Stevie has learned to use both sides of his brain at an unusually young age, he could be thought of as more like a girl in his behaviour. Using a cardigan for long hair, preferring to play with girls, dancing and enjoying expressive music are all outward features of this. However, he is even more complicated than that!

Stevie has a strong left hemisphere, allowing him to develop early language skills and an interest in people, but he also has a strong right brain, where learning and enjoyment are triggered by music, dance, drama and the arts. Stevie's hearing is also acute, unlike many young boys, who hear less well than girls throughout life, and whose ear canals tend to block up more, leaving them with temporary hearing loss and 'glue ear'. This loss affects a many as 70% of boys during their childhood, but it is neither predictable nor easy to spot. Practitioners and parents would be well advised to watch their boys carefully for unaccustomed problems with attention or listening, and have their boys' ears tested if they are suspicious. As Steve Biddulph says in *Raising Boys* (Thorsons 2003), 'Sometimes they're not naughty, just deaf!' Good hearing also makes Stevie a good mimic!

Before birth and during early childhood, boys continue to produce testosterone, and respond to its influences. Some boys produce more, and some are more sensitive to its effects, visible in their fascination with superhero play, gun play and extreme activity. However, such indicators of a testosterone 'burst' may not be apparent in some boys. These boys, and Stevie is one of them, are less sensitive to testosterone, and seem to have better ways of channelling emotions and actions. They still play imaginative games, but these are of a more gentle and expressive nature, often relying on lots of talking and emotion. They may never even get involved in the extremes of 'boy energy' play, preferring the company of other quieter children of both sexes.

Although the physical aspects of language, speaking, listening and moving, are of interest, the working of Stevie's brain has not yet motivated him to become interested in reading and writing. Our story shows that these activities never did switch this particular brain on. Despite various attempts to get him interested, these all had limited effect, and he was only motivated to do the minimum of reading and writing to get by in school. No-one is quite sure how he learned the words for his parts in play, but his listening skills would help here, and would also help us to understand why he knew the words of all the other parts too!

Key elements of the brain

In the introductory chapters of this book we explored the effect of foetal testosterone. This is testosterone released in the womb which floods the brain and body of the foetus, determining both the sex of each baby and their starting point on the gender spectrum between extreme femininity and extreme masculinity. This huge developmental lurch also affects the growth of the brain – researchers now think that sensitivity to testosterone is a genetic tendency, priming each brain cell to respond to the testosterone flood.

Generally, girls are less sensitive to the testosterone and even produce less of this substance in their bodies. In this way, they avoid the extreme effects of the foetal flood, and can continue to concentrate on brain development while their female bodies carry on growing too.

For boys, the process is more complex. They have been living in potentially female bodies too. Now they have to concentrate on changing their bodies from 'default' female mode to male, by doing such complex operations as moving their sexual organs to the outside of their bodies; developing a quite different bone structure, and making more muscle and red blood cells. During this time, the development of boys' brains appears to slow down, leaving them behind in the race towards a mature brain – a feature that haunts them for much of their childhood.

'At the age of six or seven, when children start serious schooling, boys are six to twelve months less developed mentally than girls. They are especially delayed on what are called "fine motor skills". Eventually boys catch up with girls intellectually but, in the way most schools work now, the damage is already done.' Steve Biddulph, *Raising Boys* (Thorsons 2003)

Stevie's genetic make-up seems to have provided him with a low sensitivity to testosterone, leaving his immature brain more like that of a girl. The advantage of this low sensitivity for a baby is that instead of concentrating on turning their body *and* their brain into a boy with masculine tendencies like Paul and Leroy, it is possible that Stevie and boys like him have a unique chance to continue the growth of their brains (both right and left hemispheres) while allowing their bodies to grow into boys.

Boys whose brains are more like female brains, and girls whose brains are more like male brains are *not* destined to become homosexual (although some of them may). It is now thought that one in seven females has a 'male' brain, and one in five males has a 'female' brain, and that the 'maleness' and 'femaleness' is idenitifiable at one day old! The great majority of these people follow perfectly normal lives, they just bridge the gender gap and in doing so make it impossible to make simple declarations about boys and girls, or women and men.

As children, these individuals have been described by Michael Gurian, founder of the Gurian Institute as 'bridge brains' – making the bridge between masculine and feminine characteristics, and the choices they make in their adult lives are often affected by their bridge brains. Boys and girls, women and men in this group may become artists, poets or dancers; they may follow careers in the caring professions such as nursing, teaching or social work; men may become 'stay-at-home' dads, and women may sail around the world.

We need these people, who are not at the extremes of brain or body, sexuality or gender, they are balanced in the middle. This is a great advantage as an adult, because 'bridge brains' have a wider choice of career choices, they will probably make better partners, and they will enjoy a wider range of activities than someone whose nature, nurture and chance has placed them at the extremes.

However, for some children, particularly boys, being a bridge brain may well also expose them to teasing, or to becoming what Michael Gurian calls 'underboys', in *The Minds of Boys* (Jossey Bass 2005). Girls who have sporting or adventurous spirits have a better time than boys who dance! Underboys often have a much harder time and can be teased or bullied in school or in the community, becoming stressed or distressed by something over which they have no control.

During gestation and early childhood, the left hemisphere of the brain grows and develops much more slowly than the right, both in girls and boys, and links between brain cells before birth and during the first years of life are almost all made in the right hemisphere. The right hemisphere responds well to active learning, using all the senses, and to space, colour and rhythm. This is why good early years education emphasises play and first-hand experiences. At this stage, children are not very adept at learning by being told or taught, they need hands-on learning using their whole bodies.

Girls seem to be the first to grow neural links across the corpus callosum, finding the way into the left hemisphere where order, sequence, and particularly language are processed. Stevie is one of the boys who also finds his way to the left hemisphere early. He processes language well, has a good sense of rhythm, and equally important, he is sensitive to the feelings and emotions of others as well as to his own. He is able to express himself in words and movement, and he loves music, drama and story, where he excels, using his energetic boy body. At this age, where children are less judgemental, even though he often chose to play with girls Stevie's love of life and enthusiasm made him popular with boys too.

Stevie's accepting and empathetic nature, inherited from his parents, has been reinforced by his upbringing, and he is a stable and attached boy. Thus far in his life, he has been accepted by everyone, and is confident and enthusiastic. His position on the gender spectrum and his creativity, expressed particularly in his theatrical interest, is a strength at the moment. However, our culture, our powerful media and particularly the education system all appear to value intellectual attainment over creative achievement. Children are rarely identified as gifted and talented in the arts (except if they play a musical instrument).

Despite government guidance that gifted and talented children should be identified in all areas of learning, the targets which are measured by the same government department are simply linked to reading, writing and mathematical skills. The UK Government describes the difference between 'gifted ' and 'talented' as: 'gifted' learners are those who have abilities in one or more academic subjects, like maths and English; 'talented' learners are those who have practical skills in areas like sport, music, design or creative and performing arts. (www.qcda.gov.uk/1957.aspx)

The difference between 'gifted' and 'talented' is subtle, but many people would see the first as more important than the second. We are not suggesting that Stevie is gifted in any way that could now be defined, but his creative brain may not have been recognised in the same way or held in the same high esteem as the abilities of Adam or Oliver.

So how does all this add up as we describe Stevie's 'clevernesses' and discuss his school life?

- Using both sides of the brain at an early age makes Stevie able to embark on communication more easily than many boys. His hearing is acute and he is very interested in speaking both his own words and those of others in stories and plays.

- If we could look at the structure and working of Stevie's brain, reflected in his behaviour, we would see that he is creative which is a right brain characteristic. By combining this with his strong left brain, he can imagine and invent stories, puppet shows, rhymes and 'plays' in which he is director, star, choreographer, dancer and also usually playing the lead role. He uses his social skills to explain, include (and exclude) other children at will. He then presents his story to anyone who will listen. Courtney B Cazden in *Wally's Stories* by Vivian Gussin Paley (Harvard University Press 1981) says: 'When you are five, there is much in the world that needs to be accounted for, and these accounts are "stories" to us adults when children prefer their magical explanations to those we call "true"'. Stevie's 'plays' are his version of just such explanations.

The Cleverness of Boys

- Stevie is also a very good mimic. Good hearing and sensitive auditory centres in his brain (which enable him to understand what is being heard) make him sensitive to music and tone of voice. His strong right brain also makes him visually aware. These two 'clevernesses' are essentials to mimics. Stevie picks up the mannerisms and body posture of his teachers just as accurately as he mimics their voices and speech rhythms.

- Innate creative excellence, a right brain characteristic, combined with his ability to perform confidently, even as the pieces of silver, is also clever at this age. Many children, and particularly some boys, are less confident and avoid being in the limelight, and this gets worse as they move towards adolescence. Stevie's confidence will impress other children and adults, and this will make him even more willing to perform.

- The chemical ocytocin, sometimes called the 'tend and befriend' substance, is more often found in females, but a close examination of Stevie's brain and gender balance will reveal him as one of the boys who are comfortable with girls. This is fortunate for him, as it is for girls who are comfortable with boys and will be so throughout their lives. When children are toddlers, they don't seem to know or care who are boys and who are girls, but as they begin to develop a sense of self, 'boy-ness' and 'girl-ness' become very important. Whether this is influenced by upbringing, or is cultural in a time when boys and girls are treated very differently in the clothes they wear, the toys they are encouraged to play with or the ways they behave, is impossible to tell. But Stevie is one of the lucky ones, and his gregarious nature is an asset in his primary years.

- Empathy and the ability to understand others' feelings, are more of Stevie's 'clevernesses'. He is able to relate well to adults and children, and can usually get their attention and understanding, either by strength of personality or pestering. This is a mixed blessing and has not always been seen as a 'cleverness', although it has got him far in the early years!

Other influences

Stevie's interest in people, finally finding its fulfilment in caring for the elderly, was apparent in his early years. Unlike Oliver, Stevie's ability to empathise and express his feelings in movements and words has always been encouraged by his parents, who do not see themselves as unusual, but they may seem unusual to others. They are accepting and generous-minded people, both of

South East Asian heritage, and second-generation UK citizens. They work hard to keep their shared heritage and traditions alive, while being committed to UK citizenship. Stevie's mum makes celebration cakes and sweets at home, for a local shop. His dad is a porter at the local hospital. They are neither rich nor aspiring, enjoying life to the full with what they have.

When Stevie was born, he weighed only 5lbs (normal birth weight range is between 6lbs 2oz and 9lbs 2oz), and was not very strong. He soon put on weight though because his mum had read that spending time with him and in particular, cuddling, stroking and talking to him was the best way to help his growth. What she was doing, without realising it, was helping his brain to grow too.

'Your child has a natural need to touch and be touched, listen and be listened to, smell, taste, see and be seen.' Michael Gurian, *Nurture the Nature* (Jossey Bass 2009)

Experts in childcare also say that neural development in the brain is greatly enhanced when babies are held by their parents, and that a two-month-old baby needs two hours a day of holding and human contact to flourish.

Baby massage, stories, songs and rhymes all played a part in Stevie's early development. Even when he was asleep his mother carried him in a sling as she sang or listened to music while cleaning or cooking. She has done the same for Stevie's baby sister.

Stevie's dad was also very involved in his children's early development. His shifts enabled him to be at home regularly during the day. He shared his interests with his son by reading stories in funny voices, making simple puppets and other toys, and using character voices as he played with the soft toys, play people and jungle animals that Stevie loved. When they went on walks, to Stevie's delight, he would even give silly voices to the ducks on the pond, dogs they met or the pigeons in the trees. He is bilingual and sang and spoke both languages to the children, engaging them in learning two languages, although their first language is English. Recent research has confirmed the benefits of being brought up in a bilingual family:

'Many parents and teachers still think that bilingualism can cause confusion and intellectual delay in children. In reality, there are no such drawbacks and this research shows that bringing children up bilingually could have further benefits besides being able to speak two languages.' Antonella Sorace, Professor of Developmental Linguistics (www.thersa.org/fellowship/ newsletter/issue-3/fellowship-newsletter/fellows-project-bilingualism-matters)

Before the age of five, Stevie watched very little television, and when he did see screen images, this was always in the company of one of his parents.

The Cleverness of Boys

Programmes were carefully selected and short in duration. His father had overheard discussions between doctors and other health professionals at work, and had picked up occasional magazines and newspaper articles about the effects of television on young children. Both parents are convinced that too much screen time, too early, may be harmful, another decision that makes them different from many parents, but is supported worldwide by experts in child development.

'Until we have research to the contrary, we must consider that too much viewing may change brain patterns and make it harder for a child to concentrate at school.' Jane M Healey *Your Child's Growing Mind* (Broadway 2004)

This research has now been done: 'In a new study, young children and their adult caregivers uttered fewer vocalizations, used fewer words and engaged in fewer conversations when in the presence of audible television.' Dimitri A Christakis, MD, MPH, Director of the Center for Child Health, Behaviour and Development at Seattle Children's Research Institute, 'Preschool-Aged Children's Television Viewing in Child Care Settings' in *Pediatrics* (December 2009)

Stevie's upbringing not only supported his creative mind, but protected him from some of the harmful influences that would have delayed his development.

How to recognise and value the strengths of boys like Stevie

Stevie is now an adult. If we track back to his early education, we may be able to learn some lessons for helping other boys like him, who may have difficulties in balancing their 'clevernesses' with the expectations of society and the education system. During Stevie's primary school years it was relatively easy to encourage and support his interests. Primary schools are smaller and have much more flexibility to respond to individual needs and talents. The flexible nature of the primary curriculum, and the tradition of working in stable class groups for most of the time, enables teachers and parents to be more involved in the child as a whole. A close relationship between parents and teachers is the ideal, and Stevie's parents attended parents' meetings regularly, making good relationships with all his teachers, and discussing openly their concerns for Stevie as well as their continuing pleasure in his successes.

- Engaging Stevie in reading and writing has been a constant challenge to his teachers and his parents. An upbringing in a caring and creative home did not give him the models of reading and writing for real purposes. His father was not naturally drawn to reading, and avoided writing anything. His mum also found writing and particularly maths difficult too. She usually did these activities late at night when the house was quiet.
  - After some discussion with the teachers, both parents began to raise the profile of reading and writing at home, and Stevie quickly got involved in helping his mum work out the finances of her cake-making business, by counting money, reviewing stores and making lists.
  - Boys often find reading and writing difficult and come to it later. The development of fine motor skills and use of the left brain for reading are both essentials to success, and teachers must make sure that these abilities are present before embarking on more formal activities. Government guidance such as *Confident, capable and creative: supporting boys' achievements*, (DCSF 2007) and the World Class Schools Programme announced in December 2009, was not available to Stevie's teachers, and is part of a response to a wide ranging current concern that many boys are asked to do writing and reading activities that neither their bodies nor their brains are prepared for. Pressure to do this before they are ready releases stress hormones in their brains, which may turn them off writing for life. Continuing the active nature of early years education into the primary school will also help boys like Stevie.
  - For some reluctant readers and writers, technology can be a solution. Schools today, even in their early years departments, now have access to a range of technological equipment that was not in use when Stevie was five. You can use computers, cameras, DVD and the Internet to make projects more interesting and recording in pictures and writing more enjoyable. Stevie's family bought a computer, and Stevie and his dad loved surfing the Internet, but they continued to read about the effects of too much screen time, and kept the computer in the living room where its use could be monitored.

- Like other boys in this book, Stevie is creative, and part of this ability is genetic. Supporting his involvement in and enthusiasm for drama, plays and stories was a vital part of his success in primary school, where he took part in assemblies, concerts, plays and the after-school drama club. This gave his creativity a real outlet. However, when he moved to secondary school, there were far fewer opportunities for dramatic activity, and Stevie just existed during the year, until the end-of-term productions, which he

The Cleverness of Boys

auditioned for, sometimes got a part in, and always supported backstage if he wasn't selected for acting.

It was a pity that his teachers didn't appreciate his real gifts, they just regretted that the enthusiasm he showed in dramatic activity was not reflected in academic work. Annual reports concentrated on the fact that he '...would rather sharpen pencils, make jokes and talk than get on with his work', and gave little credit to his creative ability, which of course had no measurable 'product'. This upset his parents but their loyalty to Stevie and their willingness to accept him as he was prevented them from letting him know this.

- The lesson we could all learn is that we must learn to look for strengths wherever and whatever they might be, and remember that success at exams must not be seen as the only measure.

- Boys who have a softer side are often targeted by more active, sporty and testosterone-rich boys, who may have been influenced by nurture or culture – expecting all boys to be as active and assertive as they are. In the later years of primary school, Stevie's parents began to worry about his friendship circle at school, and ask how they could widen this circle of friends beyond a group of girls and some quieter boys. The following strategies, worked well while he was in primary school:
  - His parents got involved with him in non-competitive sports. They all joined the local leisure centre where family activities are a speciality. Swimming and Family Fun days provided activities where Stevie and his family could get involved, meet other families and widen his interests. This plan had limited success in making Stevie more 'boyish' and the leisure centre membership lapsed. This was partly because of his dad's shifts, but surprisingly, Stevie, with his mum and sister, did use and enjoy the swimming pool, although it was usually early in the morning. Stevie still enjoys swimming now!
  - Stevie is unlikely to ever enjoy competitive sports or games. However, less competitive sports, where strength and control are both important, can be very enjoyable for boys with energy. These include judo, canoeing, kayaking, aerobics, recreational dance, backpacking, fishing, surfing, walking, cycling, billiards or karate. Skateboarding was the one that Stevie loved. It gave him opportunities to use his natural sense of balance and control, and he turned it into a performance art in his local park, impressing even the most masculine boys.
  - Saturday dance club was also an interest during early adolescence, and the popularity of the musical Billy Elliot and dance as a feature on

television talent programmes inspired some other boys to join too. However, the most influential boys in Stevie's group still make clear their low opinion of dance as a credible activity for boys. The audience for Stevie's dancing is now much older, but more appreciative!

- Stevie's parents may lose confidence in their style of parenting if he is teased or bullied at school or in the community. He may ask them why he is different, and what he can do to make friends or be more popular with the lads. They particularly wanted to avoid teasing and bullying when Stevie went to secondary school. Stevie's natural inclination was to work and play with more reflective children, and this sometimes resulted in a bit of gentle name-calling from boys who were previously admiring of Stevie's activities. The names 'drama queen', 'girly' and 'softy' were used in fun, but their use was worrying to everyone.
  - Stevie's parents have always encouraged him to talk about his feelings, and this is a very important skill for these boys to learn. Many boys find it difficult to talk face to face, so involve them in 'walking and talking' or 'doing and talking' to relieve the pressure of just talking.
  - Adults also need to talk about their feelings. Stevie was lucky that his parents talked about their feelings when he was young, and he learned to do so too. Primary school is a place where it's OK to talk about how you feel, but in later years it can be more difficult. The SEAL materials helped his teachers in early secondary years to give a proper place to social and emotional learning alongside the formal curriculum.
  - Bullying is a frequently used but often misunderstood word. In his book *The Minds of Boys*, (Jossey Bass 2005) Michael Gurian gives ten tips for handling bullying, the first of which is to define the term – he says: 'Teasing is not necessarily bullying, which is an attempt to physically or emotionally destroy another person'. This is a helpful way of deciding how you should react to what has happened or has been reported. Bridge brain boys can easily become 'underboys' if they have no way of talking about who they are and what is happening. Stevie's parents kept the lines of communication open at home, and a sensitive programme of personal and social education helped him at school.

Stevie is fortunate in the nature and nurture combination of his brain and body, and of the chances he has encountered during his life, particularly his teachers and his loyal group of friends. He is happy and settled in a job he enjoys, with a constant admiring audience, and a continuing close relationship with his family.

Conclusion

The boys in this book are only eight of the unique children who will pass our way. Each one is the result of a unique mixture of nature, nurture, culture and chance. Each move through education and grow up to be a unique teenager and a unique adult, and most of them will become parents, bringing their unique mixture of genes, nurture and upbringing to their own children. The success of their lives depends to a great extent on nature and chance, factors that we cannot predict or manage. However, we all have a part to play in reducing the damaging effects of the influences of nurture and culture, while celebrating their central importance in our children's lives.

As a society, we must all recognise the damage we can do by belittling the talents of boys, by stereotyping behaviours and by encouraging the worst excesses of extreme boy behaviour. We must protect our boys from the damaging effects of city streets, TV violence, gang culture and extreme risk taking encouraged in a celebrity culture, where there appear to be no limits.

As parents and grandparents, we must realise that boys are not indestructible, however strong they might seem. They are vulnerable and need our support and understanding. They need to build strong relationships within their families, so they become resilient and trusting, communicative and able to show their feelings. Only then will they be able to leave the shelter of our families and become valued members of society outside the family.

As practitioners and teachers, we need to avoid classifying boys as a homogenous group and identify each unique personality, not better or worse than girls or women, but different. The differences, should be celebrated and used as a starting point for helping boys to become confident, competent learners, not just 'less effective girls'.

If the adults in our children's lives can themselves be strong, competent, understanding and realistic, modelling the behaviours that we expect of children, there will be a chance that the boys of the 21st century will be able to make their contributions to human development through 'boy energy' alongside our newly independent and increasingly successful girls!

'..."boy energy" is one of the greatest assets of a civilisation. Our homes are built by it. Our roads are laid down in its vision. Our rocket ships fly because of it. Video games that involve on-screen physical and spatial movement are played predominantly by boys, some of whom become the race car drivers who entertain us, the mach1 pilots who challenge the known boundaries of time and space, the soldiers who protect us, the teachers, construction workers, shopkeepers and writers. Boys learn through impulsive trial and error, then become the men who as lawyers, or doctors or athletes or corporate managers, force innovation into the human theatre.'
Michael Gurian; *the Minds of Boys*

Further reading and resources

Books and articles

Baron-Cohen, Simon. (2004) *The Essential Difference*. London: Penguin Books.

Biddulph, Steve. (1997) *Raising Boys*. London: Thorsons.

Bowlby, J. (1956) *The Growth of Independence in the Young Child* in Royal Society of Health Journal 76. London: Royal Society for Pubic Health.

Building Futures – believing in children: a focus on provision for black children in the Early Years. (2009) London: Department for Children, Schools and Families.

Christakis, Dimitri A. (2009) *Watching violent TV at pre-school age linked to aggression in young boys*. www.seattlechildrens.org.

Confident, Capable and Creative: supporting boys' achievements. (2007) London: Department for Children, Schools and Families.

Effective Provision of Pre-school Education (EPPE). London Institute of Education (2007).

Fairness and Freedom: The final report of the Equalities Review. (2007) http://archive.cabinetoffice.gov.uk/equalitiesreview/upload/assets/www.theequalitiesreview.org.uk/equality_review.pdf

Gentleman, Amelia. 'Children in Care: how Britain is failing its most vulnerable' in *The Guardian* (20 April 2009).

Grant, Ian. (2008) *Growing Great Boys*. London: Vermilion.

Gurian, Michael. (2002) *Boys and Girls Learn Differently*. New York: Jossey Bass.

Gurian, Michael. (2009) *Nurture the Nature: understanding and supporting your child's unique core personality*. New York: Jossey Bass.

Gurian, Michael. (2009) *The Purpose of Boys*. New York: Jossey Bass.

Gurian, Michael with Stevens, Kathy. (2005) *The Minds of Boys*. New York: Jossey Bass.

Gutman, Leslie Morrison and Akerman, Rodie. (2008) *Determinants of Aspirations*. Centre for Research on the Wider Benefits of Learning, University of London Institute of Education.

Healy, Jane M. (1987) *Your Child's Growing Mind: brain development and learning from birth to adolescence*. New York: Broadway Books.

Independent Review of the Primary Curriculum. (2009) London: Department for Children, Schools and Families.

Learning, Playing and Interacting: good practice in the Early Years Foundation Stage. (2009) London: Department for Children, Schools and Families.

Louv, Richard. (2008) *Last Child in the Woods*. New York: Algonquin Paperbacks.

Mental Health and Growing Up: Factsheets for parents, carers and young people. Third edition 2004. London: Royal College of Psychiatrists.

National Kids' Day Survey, Luton First in *The Daily Mail*, December 2006.

National Statistics, Social Trends, No 37. London: Office for National Statistics, 2007.

Paley, Vivian Gussin. (1981) *Wally's Stories*. Cambridge, Mass: Harvard University Press.

Pinker, Steven. (2003) *The Blank Slate*. London: Penguin Books.

Pinker, Steven. (2004) 'Why Nature and Nurture Won't Go Away' in *Daedalus Magazine*.

Practice Guidance for the Early Years Foundation Stage. (2008) London: Department for Children, Schools and Families.

Schore, Allan N. (2001) 'Effects of a Secure Attachment Relationship on Right Brain Development' in *Infant Mental Health Journal 22*.

Sorace, Antonella. (2009) *Bilingualism Matters*. RSA Project Report www.thersa.org/fellowship/newsletter/issue-3/fellowship-newsletter/fellows-project-bilingualism-matters

Strachan, D.P. (1989) 'Hay fever, hygiene and household size' in *The British Medical Journal*.

Supporting parental involvement to strengthen early years attachments and encourage learning. (2009) HM Government website (www.hmg.gov.uk): New opportunities – Stengthening family life – Supporting parent involvement.

Further reading

Baron-Cohen, Simon. 'Autism: The Empathising and Systemising Theory' http://www.autismresearchcentre.com/arc/default.asp

Boyd, Hannah. (2006) 'First Grade Brain-Based Gender Differences' *Science Daily*. www.sciencedaily.com or see www.education.com/magazine/article/Gender_First_Grade

Bruer, John T. (1999) *The Myth of the First Three Years:* A New Understanding of Early Brain Development and Lifelong Learning. New York: The Free Press.

Burman, Douglas. (05 March 2008) 'Boys' And Girls' Brains Are Different: Gender Differences In Language Appear Biological' *Science Daily*. www.sciencedaily.com

Cahill, Larry. (03 March 2008) 'Sex Differences Extend Into The Brain' *Science Daily*. www.sciencedaily.com

Clarke, Jenni. and Featherstone, Sally (2008) *Young Boys and Their Writing*. A & C Black: Featherstone Education.

Claxton, Guy. (1997) *Hare Brain, Tortoise Mind*. London: Fourth Estate.

Cutting, Laurie and Clements, Amy. (18 July 2006) 'Study confirms males/females use different parts of brain in language and visuospatial tasks' *Science Daily*. www.sciencedaily.com

Featherstone, Sally and Bayley, Ros. (2005) *Boys and Girls Come Out to Play*. A & C Black: Featherstone Education.

Gopnik, Alison. (1999) *How Babies Think*. London: Weidenfeld and Nicholson.

Haier, Richard. (2005) *Men and Women Really Do Think Differently*. Live Science. www.pediatrics.uci.edu

Jossey Bass. (2008) *The Brain and Learning.* New York: Jossey Bass.

Kotulak, Ronald. (1996) *Inside the Brain.* Kansas City, USA: Andrews McMeel.

Lawrence, Peter A. (2006) *Men, Women and Ghosts in Science.* PLoS Biology, Vol 4 Issue 1. Laboratory of Molecular Biology, Cambridge. www.plosbiology.org/home.action

Moir, Anne and Jessel, David. (1992) *Brain Sex.* New York: Dell Publishing.

OECD Reports. *Understanding the Brain (2007)* and *An ABC of the Brain (2007)* and *The Pisa Report (2009).* www.oecd.org

Onion, Amanda. (2005) 'Scientists Find Sex Differences in Brain Research' ABC News Internet Ventures. abcnews.go.com/Technology/Health/story then search Amanda Onion

Pinker, Steven. (1998) *How the Mind Works.* London: Penguin Books.

Rose, Colin and Nicholl, Malcolm J. (1997) *Accelerated Learning for the 21st Century.* London: Piatkus.

Rousseau, Jean-Jacques. (1911) *Emile.* (Everyman) London, Phoenix; New Edition (1993)

Sax, Leonard. (2005) *Why Gender Matters: What Parents and Teachers Need to Know About the Emerging Science of Sex Differences.* Broadway, US: 1st Broadway Books.

Tovey, Helen. (2007) *Playing Outdoors.* Milton Keynes: Open University Press.

Worpole, Ken. (2003) *No Particular Place to Go.* Birmingham: Groundwork www.groundwork.org.uk/upload/publications/publication6.pdf

How Children lost the right to roam in four generations: www.dailymail.co.uk/news/article-462091/How-children-lost-right-roam-generations.html

Websites and other resources

Geneva Convention on Human Rights, 1948. See www.un.org/en/documents/udhr/

For videos of lectures by Steven Pinker see http://pinker.wjh.harvard.edu/

The Rhode Island State Advisory Committee on Gifted and Talented Education-www.ri.net/gifted_talented/rhode.html

Government statistics. www.statistics.gov.uk (looked after children, lone parents, ethnicity, birth weight).

Philosophy for children: www.sapere.org.uk

Gifted and talented: www.standards.dfes.gov.uk/giftedandtalented